LCCI
Testbuilder Level 1

Vicki Lywood Last

MACMILLAN

Macmillan Education
Between Towns Road, Oxford OX4 3PP
A division of Macmillan Publishers Limited
Companies and representatives throughout the world

ISBN 978-0-230-73384-8

Original design by eMC Design Ltd.
Page make-up by Xen
Illustrated by Mark Watkinson
Cover design by Jim Evoy

Author's acknowledgements
All my students who have taught me so much – John – Julian –
Thanks!

EDI is the sole source and copyright owner of the English
for Business Examination Instructions, English for Business
Examination Syllabus Topics, English for Business Examination
Assessment Format, and English for Business Examination
Marking Scheme. Macmillan would like to thank EDI for
permission to reproduce the English for Business Examination
Listening Answer Sheet.

Printed and bound in Thailand

2014   2013   2012   2011   2010
10   9   8   7   6   5   4   3   2   1

CONTENTS

∎NTRODUCTION

Welcome to TESTBUILDER: Level 1 of LCCI English for Business Tests. The English for Business tests can be taken at different levels – Preliminary, Levels 1, 2, 3, and 4. Each level builds on the previous one, and has three parts: Reading and Writing (two hours) which is compulsory; Listening (about 45 minutes) and Speaking (about ten minutes). Listening and Speaking are optional tests, although they are highly recommended to broaden your experience in the language.

LCCI Testbuilder Level 1

This book contains four practice tests for the compulsory Reading and Writing component, and two practice tests for the Listening and Speaking at Level 1. As well as the practice material, there are sections of Further Practice and Guidance attached to every question. These sections contain helpful tips and skills which can be used again and again throughout the whole of each test, and in the real test. I strongly recommend that you use them. You will find that these exercises can focus you on the material you are working with, and will help you to work more quickly, efficiently, and, above all, accurately.

Particular areas you should think about when using this book are making sure that you plan your answers accurately (especially in Question 1 of the Reading and Writing paper); that you do not 'lift' or copy directly from the task you are given; that your grammar and sentence structure is as accurate as possible; and that you give yourself enough time to finish the paper and answer all the questions. These are all things which will help you to be more successful in the test, and in the world of work.

For example, in the two hours of the compulsory Reading and Writing paper, you must:

- read through the whole paper
- plan each question
- write the answers, check your answers (using a dictionary if you wish)
- make any changes or corrections.

Two hours IS enough time to do the paper, but it is for you to plan your time in the best possible way. You need to work as efficiently and effectively so as to achieve your best possible result.

It is important to check your answers, and when you do, look out for the following things:

- you have answered the question set and followed the instructions
- your layout is acceptable and logical
- your work can be read easily
- you have spelt words correctly
- your sentences are grammatically correct.

In the tests, you may use a standard monolingual dictionary (or a bilingual dictionary if your first language is not English). Dictionaries are useful to check spellings, find the words you need, or discover the meaning of a particular word. However, it is important that you only use a dictionary when you really need to, because using one can slow you down in an examination.

Using a dictionary throughout this test book, however, will enable you to become more proficient at using it, and you will find that in the real test you will not have to use it so much anyway, if you follow the exercises and recommendations here.

How to use LCCI Testbuilder Level 1

You can use this book in two ways. The first way is to treat each practice test as a real exam, and do it under exam conditions. Time yourself, and don't refer to the Further practice section until you have completed the test. Alternatively, do the test questions together with the Further practice material. There is an Answer key which also includes information on why the answer is what it is, as well as where to find the answer in the question material.

Be ready to use a highlighter or to underline, and keep a note of where you found the answer. Also, have a notebook by your side, so you can note down any word or phrase that you think is useful, and which you may be able to use again. This will build into your own valuable reference book for you to look at again.

It is also a good idea to have a section in your notebook where you can write down the spelling of 'difficult' words, and also any words which you look up. That way, you will create your own personal dictionary which you can refer to and add to. It will be useful when you come to revise for the test itself.

For students

Use the book in the way you think is best for you: work together with a friend and plan your answers together; practise your speaking together, or check your answers before you look in the Answer key. Remember: the tips and ways of working which are suggested can be used again with different tests or exercises and make you more focused on the new task you are doing.

For teachers

Feel free to follow the book through as it is, or add your own material to it and develop other ideas which work well for your students. Above all, remember the book has been written to help students achieve their potential.

GOOD LUCK!

LCCI Level 1 Test Papers:

Reading and Writing

This qualification is for candidates who have a clear basic understanding of English in a business context. You should be able to show understanding of simple business-related communication; read, write and answer business texts and data; use office correspondence and other data to produce charts, tables, booking forms and reports; and be able to write business-style letters and memos based on information you are given.

The Syllabus

The syllabus is divided into four sections:

1 Composing a business letter or memo;

2 Business reading comprehension;

3 Information processing;

4 Text and data reformulation.

The Test

You will be given four questions. Questions 1 and 2 are worth 30 marks each, and questions 3 and 4 are worth 20 marks each. The test lasts two hours, and you are allowed to use a dictionary.

Question 1 will ask you to write a letter or memo of about 150-200 words. This could be:

- a retail order

- a customer enquiry

- a request for information

- a reply to complaints

- a reminder

- communication between work colleagues.

Question 2 involves understanding and responding to a passage of business-related prose of about 300 words. You must decide whether the statements are true or false, and provide supporting evidence. The stimulus for the exercise will be:

- a passage on a business-related topic in language appropriate to the level

- a series of statements about the content and information in the passage.

Question 3 involves a 'read and think' comprehension test, based on some graphic or numerical display with facts and figures, requiring very short answers. The stimulus for the question will be data in the form of a table or a chart relating to, for example:

- prices and charge

- facilities

- staffing details.

Question 4 involves a 'read and write' reformulation task using data to complete forms or diagrams. The stimulus for the question will be selected from:

- data or information in written notes
- a conversation about a business-related situation
- a record of a telephone message or fax.

The Instructions

Here is an example of the instructions which you will see when you open your Reading and Writing paper.

INSTRUCTIONS FOR CANDIDATES

Answer **all 4** questions.

Write your answers in the spaces provided on the question paper.

If more space is needed, use the additional sheets provided.

Write your name, candidate number and question number on each sheet and attach them to the inside of your booklet.

Cross through any rough notes.

There is credit for correct spelling, punctuation and grammar.

Check your work carefully.

You may use an English or bilingual dictionary.

The Result

You will get your result as quickly as possible. There are four grades which are based on marks for accuracy in spelling, punctuation, suitable content, tone style, length, format, and clarity. The grades are Fail, Pass, Credit and Distinction.

Listening

The Listening test is optional, but I do recommend that you take it as it will give you the chance to practise listening in the same way that you might do in a work or study environment.

The Listening test is multiple-choice, with two parts. Part 1 has ten questions where you must give the correct response; Part 2 has 20 questions based on short conversations, monologues or announcements.

The Syllabus

All the listening passages can take the form of:

- face-to-face conversations
- telephone conversations
- recorded messages
- live talks
- public announcements
- radio news and advertisements.

The following situations and topics can be covered:

- the workplace
- public business
- business travel
- personal information
- travel
- work
- business transactions
- instructions and arrangements.

The Test

You will hear the test on audio cassette/CD. The complete test will take about 45 minutes. In addition to this there will be about two minutes when you will read the instructions for the test. You will mark your answers on a special Candidate Answer Sheet which will be given to you on the day of the test.

The Instructions

Here are the instructions which you will see in the real test.

Instructions to Candidates

(a) DO NOT OPEN THIS BOOK UNTIL THE SUPERVISOR TELLS YOU TO START

(b) This is a multiple choice test. The test has **2** parts with a total of **30** questions, and takes about 45 minutes.

(c) You will listen to a series of short recordings. You will hear each listening passage once, so you must listen carefully. After hearing each recording choose the correct answer to each question and mark your choice **in pencil** on your answer sheet.

(d) Do not mark your answers in this test book – only answers marked on the answer sheet can be scored. There is no time allowed at the end of the test to go back and check your answers or make any changes.

(e) During the test use a rubber eraser to rub out any mistakes on the answer sheet.

(f) Mark only one answer for each question. If you mark more than one answer for a question (for example A and C) it will automatically be scored wrong.

(g) Do not make any other marks on the answer sheet as this could accidentally affect your score.

(h) You are **not** allowed to use a dictionary during the test.

NOW WAIT UNTIL THE SUPERVISOR TELLS YOU TO OPEN YOUR BOOK

Part 1

Instructions

In Part 1 you will hear the same question three times, with three different answers to that question.

You have to choose the correct answer, conversation A, B or C.

NOTE: The questions and the answers are **NOT** printed in your question book.

Now listen to the following example

[Recording]

The correct answer to the question

'So what do you do, what's your job?'

is conversation B

'I'm an assistant manager in a small travel company'

So you would fill in 'B' on the answer sheet.

Now look at the answer sheet and find where you should start filling in the answers for Part 1.

There are 10 questions in Part 1, questions 1-10.

Now listen for question number 1

(No printed questions for Part 1)

Part 2

Instructions

In Part 2 you will hear a short conversation or an announcement. On your question paper you have a question about the conversation or announcement, and **4** possible answers. You have to choose the correct answer.

Here is an example

Read the sample question and the 4 answers, then listen to the conversation and choose the correct answer.

Question How much does one shirt cost?

A   £10.00

B   £15.00

C   £12.50

D   £20.50

Now listen to the conversation and choose the correct answer.

[Tape recording]

The correct answer is B; one shirt costs £15.00, so you would fill in 'B' on the answer sheet.

Now look at the answer sheet and find where you should start filling in the answers for Part 2.

There are 20 questions in Part 2, questions 11-30

You have ten seconds to read each question, then you will hear the conversation or announcement.

Now look at the next page, read the first question and then listen for the conversation.

The Result

You will get your result as quickly as possible. There are four grades: Fail, Pass, Credit and Distinction.

Speaking

The Speaking test is optional but I do recommend that you take it as it will give you the chance to practise speaking in the same way that you might speak with an overseas colleague in your study or work environment, and it will certainly build your confidence. Your performance in the exam is assessed using four criteria:

- fluency

- lexis

- grammar

- pronunciation.

The examination is a 1:1 conversation with an examiner, and it is recorded. Each test takes about 20 minutes, and follows the same format. You can be sure that your test result is a good reflection of your ability because the result is moderated by EDI in the UK. The test is also linked to a European-wide recognised standard of qualifications.

The Syllabus

The English for Business Speaking Test has a commercial and business focus and you will be tested on your competence in English in that context, so the Speaking test really is an extension of the Reading, Writing and Listening tests and a valuable addition to your qualification.

There are a number of suggested subjects, one of which will be chosen by the examiner to be used with each candidate:

- Earning a Living

- Production and Sale of Goods and Services

- Trade

- Transport

- Communication

- Education

- Travel and Tourism

- Money

The Test

You are given five minutes to prepare the material, which you will be given on the day of the examination.

First, you will have a two-minute general conversation to warm up and to give you the chance to talk with the examiner about your ambitions, your career so far and why you are doing the examination.

There is then a five-minute conversation based on the prompt sheet material which you have already seen and prepared.

The Result

You will get your result as quickly as possible. There are four grades, which are based on the criteria of Fluency, Lexis, Grammar and Pronunciation. The grades are Fail, Pass, Credit and Distinction.

COMMON SKILLS

Taking examinations

Taking any kind of examination or test is always stressful, but there are things you can do to prepare which will make you feel more confident and improve your performance.

Approaching each paper

There are three papers for this LCCI Level 1 Test: Reading and Writing, Listening and Speaking. Listening and Speaking are optional but I strongly recommend that you take them – they are part of the language experience you will encounter in an English-speaking country, or in the workplace and around the world. As well as using this Testbuilder and/or studying English in the classroom, here are some ideas for preparing for each paper and improving your English generally.

Reading and Writing

Reading

- Try to have as much access to English language material as possible: the Internet, newspapers and magazines are all good sources of authentic English. Some countries publish special business-style magazines for English students which can be particularly useful.

- Read as much as you can: you won't understand everything, but look at headlines, pictures, picture captions and so on to give you clues as to the content.

- Read about things you are interested in. You are more motivated and you will be able to follow what is written much better as you already know something about the subject.

- When you are looking at a text or study book, have a highlighter or coloured pen with you so that you can underline or highlight any important pieces of information, or make a note of any words you think could be useful in other contexts.

- Note down any words you have looked up in a separate notebook. This will build into a useful reference tool for you.

- Don't be tempted to look up every word you don't know. Try to guess the meaning from the context, or from similar words. You simply won't have time to look up everything in the examination itself.

Writing

- Keep a diary in English of your day-to-day activities, or write about something that interests you: a film you have seen, for example. You don't have to show it to anyone but it will get you used to writing continuous sentences in English, rather than just answering questions or filling in exercises.

- Make a note of spelling errors which you make – write each word out correctly three times in your notebook.

- Do the same with grammar mistakes. If you are studying a course with a teacher, ask if you don't understand something. If you are studying alone, find a good grammar reference book that will help you.

- Practise writing with a similar pen to the one you will use in the examination: you must handwrite this test, and that can be tiring if you are more used to word-processing or working on a computer than writing by hand.

- Make sure your writing is as legible as possible: the examiner knows you are writing under examination conditions, but check that your writing is clear so that a word or letter cannot be mistaken for something else.

Listening

- Watch TV and films in English, and listen to the radio in English as much as you can. You won't understand every word but you will begin to get a good feel for the language.

- If you are studying in an English-speaking country, pay attention to conversations around you on the bus, on the train and so on. You will be surprised by how much you understand after only a little practice.

Speaking

- Try to take every opportunity to speak English. It will be difficult at first but you will feel really proud that you made yourself understood and you will want to try again.

- If you are studying in a classroom, it may seem strange to speak English with your friend who speaks the same language as you, but when I examine I can always spot the students who have practised more and have gained confidence in speaking English.

- This is a speaking test and examiners are not looking for a perfect grammatical response. One or two grammar slips will not make much difference, except if they actually hinder communication. Your ability to communicate is more important, so think about fluency and confidence, as well as accuracy.

Examination check-list

Before the examination:

- Get as much information about the examination as you can: past papers, relevant reference and study books, date and place of the examinations.

- Plan a regular pattern of study and stick to it.

- Get used to doing questions in a limited time.

- Take two pens, two pencils, a rubber and a ruler with you. (The pen always 'runs out' or your friend has forgotten his pencil!) The ruler is very useful when you have a data question or a chart which you need to read across or down the page.

- Remember where you have put your entry form or any other documentation which you need.

- Take the entry form or any other documentation with you.

During the examination:

- Make sure you can see the clock and note down the time you started.

- Read all the questions through so that you can begin to plan your time.

- Note how many questions you have to do and how long each one should take.

- Plan you answer to the question – this could be as simple as underlining key words or noting down ideas you want to include.

- Write the question number on the paper.

- DON'T copy out the whole question on the answer paper (the examiner knows what the question is).

- DON'T write out your answer and then copy it out again – you will not have time to complete the paper.

- Read the question again when you have finished answering it: make sure you have answered all of it.

- Check for grammar and other mistakes such as spelling and correct them clearly.

After the examination:

- You have done your best, so relax.

- DON'T look at your notes to check what you did wrong: it's too late!

- Think of all the good things you did.

- Look forward with confidence to the result.

Study Skills

As with any examination or test it is important to have the skills to help you study most effectively, and to approach tasks you have to do in a work or examination situation in the best way.

At this point, you might consider ways that make you study most effectively. For example, are you a 'night' or 'day' person: when are you at your most productive and can get your work done most efficiently and quickly? Do you work better with or without music? Do you prefer to work with another person or do you like to work on your own? Once you have answered these questions, try to study to that pattern. This will help you get the most out of your study periods.

Things to remember

- Don't study for longer than 45 minutes without a break: any longer and you are less productive, so build regular breaks into your study schedule.

- Most people can only remember five new vocabulary items at a time, so don't overload yourself with new words.

- Have the right reference material before you start: a good dictionary, a user-friendly grammar reference book, and your own notebook.

Skimming

Exercise 1

Look at the questions first, and then read the information panel on the following page. Remember that you do not have to read all the information to find the answers.

1   What is the text about?

   A The Pavilion Company

   B The Business Centre

   C Computers

2   There is no information about opening hours.

   A True

   B False

   C Unknown

3   Internet access is very expensive.

   A True

   B False

   C Unknown

4   What subjects are specialised in?

   A Economics and business management

   B Computing

   C Business

5   The Centre is always open.

   A True

   B False

   C Unknown

Pavilion plc Business Centre UK

Welcome to our Business Centre, where you will find all kinds of useful magazines, facts and figures and reference books, particularly on economics and business management.

You can also use our computers for free Internet access.

For items you cannot find, please ask at our Reception Desk.

Opening hours:

Monday-Friday 0830-1800 (Lunch time closure)

Scanning

Exercise 2

Look at the following questions first and then read the advertisement below. Remember you do not need to read every word of the advertisement in order to find the answer.

a) How old must the candidates be? _____

b) What kind of person does the company need? _____

c) How much money will you earn per hour? _____

d) How do you contact the company? _____

e) What is the reference number? _____

DERHAM COURIERS

Job opportunities

?? Between 16-65 – Need more money – work early, or late or night shifts ??

Our company needs motivated and reliable people for the next 3 months

Pay £6.50 per hour with the possibility of overtime

Contact us if you have good communication skills and experience of teamwork

Email us on: derhamcouriers@ pavilion.com

Reference: **2108**

Planning

Planning an essay answer is essential. This could be as brief as a few phrases or words with bullet points to remind you of key facts, or as complicated as 'mind-mapping': a concept in the middle of the page with lines or arrows connecting and linking to different areas to consider. Using a list of bullet points is probably the simplest way to plan an outline of a task in an examination.

Exercise 3

Imagine that you have been asked to prepare an in-house advertisement for a company training session. Think first what five key pieces of information you would have to give (e.g. Subject), and note them in the box below:

Information

1 _____

2 _____

3 _____

4 _____

5 _____

Exercise 4

Now that you have your five points, think about the additional information you might give about each of them (e.g. Subject – Working with customers), and add them to your original list. Remember to keep the information short – no more than a line for each piece.

Details

1 _____

2 _____

3 _____

4 _____

5 _____

Look in the Answer key for a model answer. How does your answer compare?

Note-taking

Note-taking is an essential skill – whether in a listening test, taking a message on the phone or noting down key points in a report.

Exercise 5

Look at this note left for you by a secretary. It is very long, but the information you require is only a few words. See if you can pick out the facts you need using no more than 15 words. I suggest you underline the key words and phrases as you scan the message.

Attention: Mr Smith

Mr Jones called today (Tuesday) and left the following message for you:

He has not been able to contact you by phone. He called you today 3 or 4 times but your secretary (me!) said you were in a meeting.

They need to speak to you about your recent order — it is very urgent and they would like you to call them back ASAP Tuesday.

Thank you.

(69 words)

Note: _____

_____

Dictionary Skills

You may often come across words you don't know in a text. Of course, you can use a dictionary, but it might be better to try and do without it, particularly when practising for an examination. Although you are allowed a dictionary in the test, it can be very time-consuming and distracting to use it.

Very often, it is possible to work out the meaning from the context, if you look at the sentences before and after the word, or if the word is repeated.

Look at the words in the box. Unless you know these words already, it's very difficult to work out their meaning.

consensus	exaggerate	gauge	omit	yield

Exercise 6

Now, look at these words in context, and see if you can make an intelligent guess as to their meaning.

a) The members of the committee discussed the matter for a long time, and finally reached a **consensus** which everyone was satisfied with.

Meaning: _____

b) Although the sales figures were good, the newspaper which reported a $10billion profit was **exaggerating**.

Meaning: _____

c) The **gauge** on the machine showed very low pressure in the pump.

Meaning: _____

d) The secretary **omitted** the most important detail in the email, so it had to be sent again, with the additional sales figures attached.

Meaning: _____

e) The average **yield** from the investment was five per cent per year, which is a good profit in the present economic climate.

Meaning: _____

If you look in a dictionary, you may often find that there is more than one meaning to the word you are looking up. For example, if you look up 'gauge' from sentence c) above, you will find that the meaning needed is the first given in the dictionary entry, but if you look up 'yield' from sentence e), you will see it is probably second place in the entry.

Remember: skim the whole dictionary entry for the meaning which best fits the context of the word that you are looking up.

Exercise 7

Find the correct form of the word in brackets and complete the sentence. Use a dictionary if necessary.

a) The customer bought 600 _____ from the baker. (loaf)

b) The farm supplied _____ to the restaurant once a month. (deer)

c) She _____ a formal dress to wear at the office party last night. (choose)

d) Can you _____ me _____ touch _____ Mr Wood? I've lost his phone number. (put +?)

e) After the sale, the shop _____ its prices, so it was really expensive to shop there. (put + ?)

Exercise 8

Look at these words and each pair of definitions. Which definition, 1 or 2, is the correct one? Look in a dictionary to check.

a) dandy   1 a common weed growing in the garden

                       2 a man who cares too much about his appearance

b) uncanny   1 unnatural, strange

                       2 unable to be done

c) belfry   1 a tower for bells

                       2 a kind of pan used in the kitchen

d) lisp   1 the sound a snake makes

                       2 the inability to pronounce 's'

e) Adam's apple   1 something which moves up and down when you speak

                       2 something mentioned in the Bible

f) fishmonger 1 a person who sells fish

                       2 a special line for catching fish

g) prissy   1 a pet-name for a girl

                       2 excessively neat and tidy

Exercise 9

Sometimes a word has two or more meanings or can be used as both a verb and a noun. Can you understand these sentences? Use your dictionary if you need to.

a) The carpenter accidentally nailed the nail through his nail.

b) He parked next to the park.

c) I saw him saw the wood with his saw.

d) The girl with the wavy hair waved as she disappeared under the waves.

e) The little boy was trying to tie his tie.

Exercise 10

Which word is wrong in each sentence? Underline it and write the correct spelling. All the wrong words have the same pronunciation as the right ones.

a) The assent of Mount Everest was sponsored by a well-known bank.

   _____

b) I ate a pair salad at our business lunch.

   _____

c) 'Please repair the souls and heels on these shoes,' said the customer.

   _____

d) The ship was tied to the boy in the harbour.

   _____

e) She used some flower to make a cake which became our most successful product.

   _____

f) A hair usually has long ears.

   _____

g) The driving school car had duel controls, so the instructor could stop the car if necessary.

   _____

h) The rain of the king was the longest in the country's history.

   _____

Remember: you can sometimes work out the meaning of a word by looking at its beginning (prefix) and ending (suffix).

The test papers: practice

Reading and Writing

Question 1 of the Reading and Writing paper asks you to write either a letter or a memo of between 150-200 words, based on information given to you. Here we will look at a memo.

Consider what a memo is used for. It's usually less formal than a letter, and might be used to communicate information about something within a department or office. It might contain a reminder about something – perhaps an event or meeting, or something you are expected to do. It is almost certainly communication between colleagues rather than to a customer or another company.

Exercise 11

Look at the example question on the following page. How is a memo different in layout from a letter?

_____

Exercise 12

Who is the memo communicating between here?

_____

Exercise 13

Look carefully at who you are in the scenario, and then consider the attitude you will adopt. Highlight the words and phrases which give you some clues about your attitude and style.

Exercise 14

What is the memo asking about? What are the four keys points which are needed? Are there any other points which need to be included?

_____

_____

Exercise 15

It is important that you don't 'lift' from the information you are given, and that you write in your own words as much as possible. Look at these phrases from the task below and see if you can rewrite them in your own words.

a) how far advanced the arrangements are _____

b) the timetable for the day _____

c) the visitors will be seeing _____

d) coffee and lunch arrangements _____

e) you are available on the day_____

f) you consider this matter very important _____

Exercise 16

Write the memo in the answer box. When you are finished, look at the model answer in the Answer key. How did you do?

Question 1

You are employed as the Manager of a local sportswear company, and you are looking for new customers. The company has organised an 'open day' when representatives of various sports clubs and shops will be visiting you to look at your products and discuss possible contracts.

Task

Write a memo of between 150-200 words to your Deputy Manager, who is in charge of organising the visit. Check how far advanced the arrangements are, and ask him for a provisional programme. Also find out about the following points:

* the timetable for the day

* which Departments the visitors will be seeing

* who the visitors will be talking to

* coffee and lunch arrangements

Make sure he knows your availability on that day, and that you want information from him as soon as possible, as you consider this matter very important.

Write your **memo** in the space below.

┌───┐
│   **MEMORANDUM**   │
│   TO: │
│   FROM: │
│   DATE: │
│   SUBJECT: │
│   │
│   │
│   │
│   │
│   │
│   │
│   │
│   │
│   │
└───┘

Question 3

This question is a combination of reading and thinking and usually involves some kind of graphical or numerical data. There will be 20 questions, all of which require very short answers. The key to this question is not to be distracted by the amount of data you are given.

It is important to look carefully at the questions first so that you have them in your mind when you look at the material. Skimming and scanning techniques are essential to help make sense of the material and save you time.

First, look at the questions below. You will see that the context is finance, but you should not worry if you do not have a financial background: the purpose of this exercise is for you to find information by skimming and scanning, not to do difficult financial calculations or show knowledge about economics or the financial markets. All the answers to the questions are given on the page.

Remember: the answers you need are a single word, a name or a figure, not complex information or a long sentence.

Exercise 17

The questions which you are asked are designed to have a fact or piece of information as the answer, and so most of the questions will begin with a question word, such as 'which' or 'who'. To make this exercise easier, I have grouped the questions together by question word, although this wouldn't happen in the real exam. Look at the task on page 19 and answer the following questions.

a) Questions 1-8 are all 'which market(s)' questions. What is the type of answer which will be required here? Is it a number or a name?

_____

b) Questions 14-16 are all 'how many markets' questions. What type of answer is required here?

_____

c) Questions 18-20 all say 'name the market'. What type of answer is required here?

_____

You work for a financial magazine. This week you will be looking at the World Share Market with your colleagues. You have to make sure you can answer all their questions.

Task

Study the information in the table headed World Share Markets, then answer the questions below. Write your answers as a single word, a name or a figure. You will lose marks for unnecessary information.

ANSWER

1 Which market has the biggest change on the week?

2 Which market has the lowest level at present?

3 Which market is at a 12-month high over 20000?

4 Which market shows a current level below 10?

5 Which market's results are all in single figures or fewer?

6 Which markets have current levels just over 8000?

7 Which is the market with the most consistently high figures quoted?

8 Which 2 markets have a current level between 3000 and 3500?

9 What is the Dow Jones World 12-month low?

10 What is the biggest 12-month low?

11 What is the name of the market with the 12-month high of 297?

12 What is the Australian market's change this week?

13 What are the names of the Dow Jones markets?

14 How many different markets are quoted for the FTSE?

15 How many Share Markets use numbers in their names?

16 How many markets have a 12-month high over 25000?

17 How often are the share changes given?

18 Name the market which uses percentages.

19 Name the market which has fallen by almost 700 over 12 months.

20 Name the only market with a + change this week.

Now look at the table below. Notice how it is laid out: this will help you find the answers to the questions more quickly.

Exercise 18

a) Look carefully at the titles across the page. What are they?

_____

b) Look carefully at the list on the left. What are they the names of?

_____

Exercise 19

a) How many figures use a minus (-)? Which column are they in?

_____

b) How many names of Share Markets also have numbers with them?

_____

c) A number of well-known cities are mentioned. What are they?

_____

WORLD SHARE MARKETS	Change On Week	Current Level	12-mth High	12-mth Low
FTSE 100	-401	4147	6376	3781
FTSE A/S Yield %	-3	4	6	3
FTSE All Share	-147	2079	3243	1890
Dow Jones Industrial	-317	8281	13136	7449
S&P 500	-40	850	1440	741
Nasdaq Composite	-42	1529	2551	1295
Toyko Nikkei 225	-606	8230	14489	7162
Frankfurt Dax	-417	4366	7314	4127
Paris Cac 40	-282	3016	5142	2881
FTSE Eurofirst 300	-61	805	1506	760
Hang Seng	-1121	13255	26262	11015
Australia All Ords	-185	3494	6035	3332
Dow Jones World	-10	162	297	143
Bombay Sensex	-82	9323	19013	8451
Shanghai Composite	+49	1954	5180	1706

Exercise 20

Now do the task itself.

Listening

The Listening test is in two parts. Part 1 gives you three responses to a question you will hear on the recording – you are not shown the question – and you have to choose the most appropriate response. Part 2 gives you the question and four possible answers. Using information you hear on the recording, you have to choose the best answer to the question.

Look at this Part 1 question, given to you here in full with both the question and the responses.

1   Where are you studying?

   A I'm doing some exams at the moment.

   B I'm finishing my course soon.

   C I'm studying at City College.

Exercise 21

Look at the question word in the question. What kind of response is required?

_____

Exercise 22

Although all the responses relate to the topic of study, only one gives the answer to the word 'where'. What is the correct answer?

_____

Exercise 23

Now look at the other responses and write questions which would give those answers.

a) _____

b) _____

Do the same for the two other questions which follow. Be careful with question 3, where the question does not contain a question word.

Exercise 24

2   When is the last bus to the station?

   A 2315

   B From bus stop 81

   C It costs 1.60.

Correct answer: _____

Question 1: _____

Question 2: _____

Exercise 25

3   Can I buy my ticket here?

   A Sorry, I don't know the cost.

   B Yes. Where would you like to go?

   C No, I've lost my ticket.

Correct answer: _____

Question 1: _____

Question 2: _____

Exercise 26

Here is an example of a Part 2 question. What kind of information is required? Which answer, A, B, C or D, do you think is the answer?

---

1   What can you buy cheaply in the shops at this time of year?

   A Electrical items

   B 10% off

   C No charge for delivery

   D Good things

Exercise 27

Look at the transcript below. What other information are you given which could distract you from the correct answer?

Interviewer: Tell us about bargains in the shops now.

Expert: Shopping is still expensive, but looking in shops on the High Street will help you find some good bargains in TVs, DVD players. Furniture such as sofas have 10% off at the moment and are often delivered free.

Exercise 28

Read the following question and transcript. What is the answer? What other information might distract you?

2   What was positive about Williamson's last year?

   A More people went on holiday.

   B Fuel costs were the same.

   B New planes were delivered.

   D Profits were slightly better.

News Reader: … Williamson's results are just in. Increased passenger numbers meant that the planes delivered last year were used to capacity, and the cost of fuel decreased, resulting in an improved profit on last year of £10m.

If you want to practise further, all the transcripts for all Part 1 and Part 2 questions in the two complete Listening Tests are on pages 115-119.

Speaking

Taking the first step to speak in a foreign language is the most difficult one, but the sense of satisfaction and the gradual building of confidence will make it worthwhile. As an examiner, it is always clear to me which students have practised speaking in English, and which students have continued to avoid it. Learning and speaking another language is exciting – you learn about different ideas, new concepts and you meet people. Throughout the book there are many exercises and suggestions for things to talk about with other students taking this qualification, or to discuss with colleagues. Please take the opportunity to use them!

PAPER 1 READING AND WRITING 2 hours

QUESTION 1

Situation

You work in the delivery department of ODDS Tools. You have recently received an order for some new equipment to be supplied to one of your oldest customers, DBC Manufacturing. The delivery of this equipment has been delayed because of difficulties shipping it from your factory overseas.

Task

Write a letter of between 150 and 200 words to your customer including the following:

- a confirmation of receipt of the order
- an explanation of the reason for the delay
- a statement as to when the equipment will be delivered
- an offer of a (small) discount because of the delay.

You should remember that DBC Manufacturing is a very important and valued customer.

Write your **letter** in the space below.

(30 marks)

QUESTION 2

Situation

You are preparing for an interview with Kleinco. You have received some background information about the history of the company.

Task

Read the article below entitled "THE MENNCO STORY", then say whether the statements which follow are **TRUE or FALSE.** Then **quote** the words or phrases from the article that support your answer. Do **not** write more than 6 supporting words for each answer. You will lose marks if you write more than this.

Note: Answers are usually in 2 parts. You may need to look in different places in the article to find the supporting words you need.

Example:

Statement: The Company's name is Men and Co and it started in the 1600s.

Answer: FALSE   Menn and Co/established 1971

THE MENNCO STORY

Menn and Co was established in 1971 by father-and-son team Irvine and William Menn. Irvine had a background in accountancy and finance, while William was the 'design genius'. The company has played a major part in the development of space research in recent years, co-operating with NASA on some of its most exciting projects, having started out as a company specializing in electronic engineering.

Menn and Co found almost instant success, due to its new and imaginative ideas and state-of-the-art equipment design. It quickly expanded to employ almost a thousand skilled and unskilled workers. Factories were established first in the UK and then in France (where a local Director was appointed), and Hong Kong.

In 1990, when Menn senior died, William became Managing Director and Chief Executive of the company, although he still spent considerable time in the design department, where he worked on many of the company's famous products. Now retired, he still acts as a much-valued consultant from time to time.

The company's name was slightly changed to Mennco in 1984, to give it a more 'modern' feel. Since then, the company has diversified into other areas of engineering. Household and small technical equipment, in particular, have had considerable success and popularity in the marketplace.

Some problems have been experienced over the last decade due to the general economic situation in Europe, which has meant that the French operation is now controlled directly from the UK, but job cuts have been avoided so far.

Mennco is proud to say that control of the company still remains within the Menn family. It sees a bright future for the company, having recently won an award for original design. Next year sees the fortieth anniversary of the foundation of the company and a number of special events are planned for this, but Mennco is not yet going to reveal what they are. It is certain, however, that consumers and markets will not be disappointed with these events, or with the company's performance.

Write your answers on the lines marked A.

1 Mennco is a well-known company and has something to celebrate.

A —————————————————————————————————

2 It is a family company; the family is still involved in its work.

A —————————————————————————————————

3 Mennco makes one product which is only available in the UK.

A —————————————————————————————————

4 The company employs workers internationally in different roles.

A —————————————————————————————————

5 The company's name changed because of Irvine's death; now the family has no control over it.

A —————————————————————————————————

6 Economic problems have caused job cuts.

A —————————————————————————————————

7 Product design has always been important; the company has won prizes for its designs.

A —————————————————————————————————

8 The company developed slowly and has small factories.

A —————————————————————————————————

9 William Menn is the Managing Director and Chief Designer today.

A —————————————————————————————————

10 The company is ignoring its anniversary next year; it is establishing a theatre.

A —————————————————————————————————

(30 marks)

QUESTION 3

Situation

You work for a website which compares new products from car manufacturers. You are looking at 4 new cars recently released by DDD Motors.

Task

Study the information in the table below, then answer the questions on the next page. **Write your answer as a single word, a name or a figure in the answer column.**

AWA PRODUCTS 2010-2011

PRODUCT NAME	(£) PRICE	(£) SAVING	DETAILS
TIGER	7,795	1,590	CD player central locking manual petrol
VERON	12,445	1,545	CD player climate control 16″ alloy wheels manual/automatic petrol/diesel
VENTURE	13,545	3,815	satellite navigation climate control CD player manual/automatic petrol/diesel
TOURER	14,595	2,175	7 seat + flat seat system CD player satellite navigation manual/automatic diesel/liquid petroleum gas

ANSWERS

1   Which car has the biggest saving?

2   Which car has specialized seating?

3   How many cars have CD players?

4   What is special about the Veron?

5   Which is the most expensive vehicle?

6   Which car has the fewest extras?

7   How many cars use diesel fuel?

8   What is the price of the cheapest car?

9   Which two cars have air-conditioning?

10   What is the name of the car probably most suitable for a family?

11   What type of fuel does the Venture use?

12   What is the Tiger's extra security detail?

13   What is unusual about the Tourer's fuel?

14   How many cars have satellite navigation and climate control?

15   Which car has the smallest saving?

16   Is it possible to play tapes in any of the cars?

17   Which car has one type of gear-shift?

18   How many cars use only diesel?

19   What is the size of the Veron's wheels?

20   Which car has the smallest number of features?

(20 marks)

QUESTION 4

Situation

You are the organizer of an international meeting, to be held at the London office of your company. You have received the following messages about changes to the arrangements of some of the delegates.

1

Kicki Backman called from Gothenburg. She will be arriving as planned on flight SAS 707 and should arrive in London at about 1830. However, she has changed her hotel booking, to be in the same hotel as her colleague. She will be staying at the Grand Hotel, not the Gregory in Oxford Road. She can be contacted on 07743 112233 after 2000.

2

There was also a phone call from France. Anne Smith's flight will now be to Manchester, where she will arrive at about 2000. She will probably not get to her hotel in London until about 2330. She is planning to stay at the Great Western Hotel, but asked if we could phone them to say she will be arriving late. If you need to speak her, it's best to speak to her colleague at the hotel – Room 333.

3

Mr Wood will be coming back by train from Manchester. He will arrive at 1500, and is not now staying at the Metropole Hotel. He has changed his reservation to the Oak Tree Hotel in Mansfield Road. Julian can be contacted by email, or in an emergency please contact his secretary. (You should have her number already).

4

Finally, there was a phone call from John Cox in Stockholm. He wanted to check that we had changed Ms Backman's hotel booking – the Grand Hotel. He will be arriving later than her, at about 2000 on flight 787. He's available until tomorrow only by email, and then at the hotel, so please contact them if it's urgent.

Task

Use the information above to complete the table below.

DELEGATES' ARRANGEMENTS

(Complete in capitals)

Name of delegate	Flight	Arrival time in London	Hotel	Contact details
1				
2				
3				
4				

(20 marks)

QUESTION 1

Look carefully at the question given, and decide on the style it is best to have when you write this letter. What kind of style should you use? Think about the person you are writing to (the target reader). For example, if you wrote to your friend, you might begin with 'Hi!' and use lots of informal words and contractions (short word-forms). On the other hand, a letter to a Manager might begin 'Dear Sir' with no contractions or informal words.

Exercise 1

Look at examples 1-3 of the beginnings of letters. Which one do you think is:

a) to a friend? _____

b) to an elderly relative? _____

c) to a bank manager? _____

1   Dear Aunt Florence

Thank you for your recent birthday wishes and cheque. I am most pleased to receive your greetings.

2   Hi there!

Hope you're OK. It was really great to meet up last weekend. The film was fantastic, wasn't it?

3   Dear Mr Smith

Thank you for your letter. I will be pleased to come and see you to discuss my account. I will phone today in order to make an appointment.

Note the information you are given about the **type** of customer J I Manufacturing is, and then choose which style of writing it would be better to use.

Exercise 2

Looking at the four task points you must include in your letter, think about ways of expressing them clearly.

a)   How can you confirm you have received their order?

_____

b)   Why might something be delayed?

_____

c)   Think of a suitable date for something to be delivered.

_____

d)   How much money or what kind of offer might be suitable?

_____

For all these points, think of your own experience, and perhaps discuss it with another class member or friend. This discussion might be useful for your Speaking Test.

Have you ever had a problem with a company or shop? What happened? For example, did you complain or was there a problem with the service?

What offers have you seen advertised? For example, '2 for the price of 1'; prices reduced for a short time only; something free if you buy something else.

Which would you prefer – cheaper prices or better service? Why?

Exercise 3

Look at the model answer on page 31. Are there any words you might have difficulty spelling? For example, look in the first paragraph. Can you find a word which begins with 'r' and means saying that you have got something from someone?

_____

Exercise 4

Try to find other words which have 'ei' in the middle. Here are a few clues to help you:

a) The word means 'not from the same country'.   _____

b) The word means 'very strange'.   _____

c) The word means 'something over your head in a house'.   _____

It is a good idea to keep a separate spelling notebook, where you note down useful words which you find in your reading, and which you can re-use in your writing. If you have problems remembering them, write them out three times and you will find you gradually get the spelling right every time.

Exercise 5

Here are five other words which it will be useful to learn in a business context. Can you decide which ones are correct, and which ones you need to correct? Clue: only two are correct. Write the correct spelling where necessary.

a) address _____   b) approximatively _____   c) seperat _____

d) permanent _____   e) reccomend _____

Exercise 6

Read the model letter. There are some words and phrases which it might be useful to make a note of, for use in other letters or exercises you might have to do.

See if you can find words and phrases which mean the same as those below. The number of words you need to find is in brackets.

a) I am sorry to tell you (6 words)

_____

b) We hope it is OK (5 words)

_____

c) … sent now (3 words)

_____

d) In order to do something nice (5 words)

_____

e) If you want to talk more about this (8 words)

_____

Question 1

Model Answer

ODDS Tools Manchester Street London NZ 03B

5th March 2009

Mr Smith
DBC Manufacturing
Sterling Road
Leeds LE7 9BS

Dear Mr Smith

We are very pleased to confirm receipt of your recent order for 300 examples of Machine Tool No 5014, which arrived on 03.03.09.

Unfortunately, I have to inform you that this particular model has been in short supply recently, due to some minor production problems in our supplier's factory, which, as you know, is situated in Finland. The company has now resolved this problem.

We are able to offer 150 examples of the model for immediate despatch, with the remainder guaranteed to follow in no later than 3 weeks.

We hope this is suitable for you. As a gesture of goodwill, we would be happy to offer you a discount of 15% on your next order.

We hope this will be satisfactory, and look forward to continue working with you in the future.

Please do not hesitate to contact me if you wish to discuss this matter further.

Yours sincerely

ODDS Tools

(159 words)

Exercise 7

What do you notice about the language in the letter? Is it like everyday speech, or is it quite formal using quite long phrases and unusual words?

Question 2

Always remember to use a highlighter or underline when you prepare to do this kind of exercise.

Skills: skimming and scanning

Look first at the statements given and read them quickly (**skim**). Then highlight or underline any words or types of words which you think are similar. For example, paragraph 1: established = started out.

Then read the text, and highlight or underline any words or phrases which seem to 'connect' with the statements which you have already read. For example, paragraph 1: specialising in = question 3: makes one product.

Look back at the statements for a second time, and then reread the text looking carefully (**scan**) – at what you have highlighted – for the information you need to answer each question. For example, paragraphs 3 and 4 = question 5.

Always use this technique – you will become quicker at it, and it will make you more accurate in your reading skills.

Exercise 8

Find as many names or place-names as you can and highlight or underline them.

Exercise 9

Find as many dates or numbers as you can and highlight or underline them.

Remember that some of the statements given will be false, and you must select information to confirm the statement (T) or disagree with the statement (F). Only select a maximum of six words for each statement.

Exercise 10

Look at these questions, and see if you can answer them with just a word or a few words from the text in two minutes:

a) What was William known as?

_____

b) Why was the company successful so quickly?

_____

c) What does William do now?

_____

d) What happened in 1984?

_____

e) What has not happened so far?

_____

f) What is the future for the company?

_____

Question 3

This exercise is testing your ability to read quickly and accurately. Skimming and scanning techniques will help you here.

Exercise 11

You have 20 questions to answer, which all relate to a limited amount of information. Which do you think it is better to look at first – the questions or the text? What would it be helpful to do as you skim read for the first time?

_____

Exercise 12

Consider **what** type of questions are being asked, for example, do you have to choose the answer (a or b or c or d) or are you being asked to pick out just one fact?

For example, some questions want you to find two names (question 9) and some questions want just a number (question 1).

_____

Grammar: | *asking questions* |

Note the different ways the questions are asked: almost all questions begin with a question word – *what/how/which* but question 16 needs a *yes/no* answer with a piece of information to support the answer.

Exercise 13

Read these *wh*-questions, then answer them.

a) Where do you live? _____

b) What do you do? _____

c) When do you start work? _____

d) Who do you work for? _____

e) Why do you work there? _____

Exercise 14

a) There is a similar verb construction in each question. What is it?

_____

b) How would you change it for *he* or *she* instead of *you*?

_____

Exercise 15

Using the examples from exercise 13, write questions using *she* instead of *you*.

a) _____

b) _____

c) _____

d) _____

e) _____

Exercise 16

Look at the following questions. They are called *yes/no* questions or closed questions, because the answers are limited. For all these questions you might reply 'Yes, I do' / 'No, I don't', or 'Yes, I am' / 'No, I'm not'. Write your own answers.

a) Do you live in England? _____

b) Are you a teacher? _____

c) Do you start work at 0800? _____

d) Are you at work now? _____

Exercise 17

Look back at the information you are given in the table on page 26.

a) Which two features are the same? _____

b) Which four features are mentioned only once? _____

Clue: Look at wheels and technical equipment.

Grammar: | *superlatives* |

Look at questions 1, 5, 6, 8, 15 and 20 on page 27. All these questions have superlative words in them. For example, question 1 asks for the BIGGEST saving. In order to form superlatives, it is important to know how many syllables there are in the adjective you want to use. A syllable is one 'sound part' of a word. For example, in the word 'syllable' there are 3 syl-la-ble(s).

Exercise 18

Look at the table below, and answer the following questions.

Adjective	Superlative adjective
old	oldest
cheap	cheapest
big	biggest
thin	thinnest
fat	fattest
late	latest

a)   How many syllables are there in each of the adjectives in the first column? _____

b)   What do we add to the adjective to make it superlative? _____

c)   What do we add to an adjective which ends in 'g', 'n' or 't'? _____
___

d)   What do we add to an adjective which ends in 'e'? _____

Exercise 19

Now look at this table and answer the following questions.

Adjective	Superlative adjective
narrow	narrowest
simple	simplest
happy	happiest
intelligent	most intelligent
good	best
bad	worst

a)   How many syllables are there in each of the first three adjectives? _____

b)   How many are there in 'intelligent'? _____

c)   What do we add to adjectives with three or more syllables? _____

d)   What do we add to an adjective which ends in 'y'? _____

'Best' and 'worst' are irregular superlatives, and you will need to memorize them.

Note: when we have adjectives ending in -*ing*, -*ed*, -*ful*, or -*less* it is usual to add 'most' to them. For example 'most tired' and 'most careful'.

Exercise 20

Using the information you have just studied, correct these sentences.

a)   He is the most old boss I have worked for. _____

b)   She is the intelligentest secretary in the company. _____

c)   He is the goodest worker in the Department. _____

d)   This is the simpleest form to fill in. _____

Exercise 21

Using the prompts below, write full superlative sentences. For example, 'My boss/bad/typist in the office' would be 'My boss is the worst typist in the office'.

a) My office/large/in the building. _____

b) This idea/practical/solution. _____

c) This product/expensive. _____

d) The sales report/bad/this year. _____

Question 4

Look at the table you are being asked to fill in, and notice there are only five details for each person. Notice too that the table is in the same order as the information you are given (see the numbers 1/2/3/4), so that Box 1 refers to delegate 1 and so on.

Exercise 22

Which three details required might have numbers in the answer?

_____

Exercise 23

Look at the text itself. Find the following numbers and what they relate to – they are not necessarily in the same order as the text. Clue: two of them relate to planes, one is to do with a hotel, and one is a phone number.

a) 707 _____

b) 07743 112233 _____

c) 787 _____

d) 333 _____

Exercise 24

Who or what do these times relate to?

a) 2000 _____

b) 1500 _____

c) 2330 _____

Exercise 25

Who is staying at the following hotels? Be careful here, one hotel is not used.

a) Grand Hotel   _____

b) Gregory Hotel   _____

c) Great Western Hotel   _____

d) Oak Tree Hotel   _____

Exercise 26

With your highlighter, mark the different countries and cities in each of the paragraphs. Some paragraphs have more than one country or place.

Grammar: the future

Exercise 27

In English, we have many ways of showing future time. In this text, there is one way which is used most often. Look carefully at each of the paragraphs and see if you can find the verbs 'in the future'. What do they all have in common?

_____

Exercise 28

Look at the information below, then complete the text using the verbs in brackets in the correct future form.

The future	Form	Use
I'm meeting my friend for dinner.	present continuous	an arrangement made with others, or something happening in the near future
I'm going to work late tomorrow.	'to be' + 'going to' + verb without 'to'	a plan
I think I'll work late tomorrow.	'will' + verb without 'to'	sudden decision; something likely to happen
I work late on Mondays.	present simple	timetable; regular or formal event

At my office on Fridays, we _____ (plan) our work for the following week. Next

week I _____ (fly) to Rome for an important business conference, which the boss

asked me to attend. I _____ (meet) two important customers and I am sure it

_____ (be) very interesting.

Exercise 29

Find the following words in the text on page 28. There is one word you must find in each paragraph.

a) The word means 'get in touch with'.   _____

b) The word means 'someone you work with'. _____

c) You do this when you book a room or flight. _____

d) This means 'something is very important'.   _____

PAPER 1 READING AND WRITING 2 hours

QUESTION 1

Situation

You work in the Human Resources (HR) Department of a company. The complaints department is going to have an in-house training day soon, to improve its service to customers.

Task

Write a memo of between 150 and 200 words to members of the complaints department about the arrangements for the day, including the following:

- the date, time and place of the training
- the reason for the training
- a brief outline of the day's timetable, including coffee and lunch breaks.

You should make it clear that attendance is compulsory, even though the training day will be held on a Saturday.

Write your **memo** in the space below.

MEMORANDUM

TO:
FROM:
DATE:
SUBJECT:

(30 marks)

QUESTION 2

Situation

You work for Strong's Investment Bank and have been invited to a conference to promote banking in the UK. You have been asked to write an article about the bank, to be published in a brochure for the delegates.

Task

Read the article below entitled "STRONG'S BANK – A PROFILE", then say whether the statements which follow are **TRUE or FALSE.** Then **quote** the words or phrases from the article that support your answer. Do **not** write more than 6 supporting words for each answer. You will lose marks if you write more than this.

Note: Answers are usually in 2 parts. You may need to look in different places in the article to find the supporting words you need.

Example:

Statement: Strong's Bank has many branches and started 5 years ago.

Answer: FALSE   limited number/over many years

STRONG'S BANK – A PROFILE

Strong's Bank has seen enquiries about its accounts double in the last 5 years, perhaps because of its reputation as the 'safest bank' in the world. Last year there was a 21% increase in customer deposits, which now total more than £1.5 billion.

Why is the bank so sound? Over many years it has concentrated on security, rather than on growth. It has only a limited number of branches, too, in order to reduce overheads and maximize profitability.

Strong's Bank prides itself on the fact that customers can talk to a real person after just two rings on the phone. Its managers know their customers and remember the details of their business affairs.

Of course, nothing is free, so customers who have £15,000 or less in their accounts must pay a charge of £40 per month as well as 70p for every transaction. However, these are considered nominal charges for the personal investment service which is provided.

Pre-tax profits until March 2009 were recorded as £17.3 million, which, although not vast, is soundly invested in safe bonds and securities; the Bank's policy is one of 'cautious investment'.

Until recently, Strong's relied on recommendations from existing clients for most of its new customers, but it is now preparing to enter the market in a more conventional way. We are sure that traditional services, combined with forward-thinking, will tempt many new customers to join us.

Strong's Bank also has internet banking, with state-of-the-art security. Each of our customers is given an electronic key with a memory stick and a password. There is also a recently upgraded interactive website.

Please come and talk to our representatives during this conference and find out what Strong's personal banking and investment service can do for you.

Write your answers on the lines marked A.

1   Strong's Bank has many interested customers; it has seen an increase in money held in recent
     years.

A   ———

2   The bank has a solid foundation and limited expansion.

A   ———

3   It offers telephone banking only, with an automated service.

A   ———

4   The bank offers free accounts, but clients must save £40 a month.

A   ———

5   Profits were recorded as over £1billion, with no investments in bonds.

A   ———

6   Customers don't know the bank's managers, and the managers don't know the customers.

A   ———

7   Profits are invested in paintings, which are held securely.

A   ———

8   The bank offers computer services, with tailor-made advice.

A   ———

9   There were no profits up to March 2009; profits have been wasted.

A   ———

10   Representatives from the bank are at the conference to give delegates advice.

A   ———

(30 marks)

QUESTION 3

Situation

You work for a large, online discount computer company. An end-of-the-year sale is coming up, and you have been asked to supply details of any computers you currently have in stock.

Task

Study the information in the table below, then answer the questions on the next page. **Write your answer as a single word, a name, or a figure in the answer column.**

COMPUTERS ONLINE

PWC*	IMPR
T3200 processor 1 GB memory 120 GB hard drive 15.6" widescreen Built-in webcam £322.96	T3200 processor 2 GB memory 160 GB hard drive 17" widescreen Built-in webcam + free phone £369.97
Ref. 224 * Limited stock	Ref. 503
HH	HH Extra*
T3200 processor 3 GB memory 250 GB hard drive 15.6" widescreen Built-in webcam Discount if purchased this week £399.99	'Duo' processor 3 GB memory 250 GB hard drive 19" widescreen Wireless connectivity Webcam Graphics card £599.97
Ref. 509	Ref. 353 *3-week delivery

ANSWERS

1   Which 2 computers have 3 GB memory?

2   What is the size of the largest screen?

3   What is the most expensive price?

4   Which computer can be connected without cables?

5   Which computers have the same screen size?

6   What is the name of the HH Extra's processor?

7   How many computers have built-in webcams?

8   How much memory does the IMPR have?

9   Which computer can customers not take away?

10   The reference numbers of which computers are similar?

11   How many computers cost less than £350?

12   What is HH Extra's additional feature?

13   What problem might there be in obtaining a PWC computer?

14   Which computer has a 160 GB hard drive?

15   What is the free gift with the IMPR?

16   What type of processor is used with the HH computer?

17   What is the reference number of the HH Extra computer?

18   What is the screen size of the HH Extra computer?

19   How much does the IMPR's phone cost?

20   What is offered with the HH computer this week?

(20 marks)

QUESTION 4

Situation

You are a Human Resources Assistant in a large company. You have been given some notes about 4 candidates who were recently interviewed for a post in the company.

1

First candidate is very suitable for the job. She is 24, and studied French and Business at London University. She's been working in marketing for about 2 years, I think, including 6 months in Paris. Her name is Ann Warwick. I think she's away on a trip now, but we can get hold of her on 00127 721721 after Tuesday.

2

Brian Macintosh was also quite well-qualified. He has a lot of experience – 5 years in Europe and another 2 years in China, so he's a bit older than Ms Warwick – 35. He studied International Relations at university, and because of his work abroad he speaks quite good Chinese (useful for us with our branch in Shanghai?) and French, with some German. He's moving house at the moment, but he gave me his email address, which is britm@pavillon.com.

3

Next interviewee was late, so we were not very impressed by that! Educated in Scotland – at Glasgow University – he speaks a little Portuguese. Name was Jonathan Baker, and he said he was 27 (although he looked older!). Can contact him at his mother's address – phone 020 333 1112. Has worked abroad for 3 years after university and has only just returned to the UK.

4

Probably the weakest candidate we saw today. Name was Helen Rawlings. Studied in South Africa and then came to the UK to do a Masters in Business Administration at Durham University. She doesn't have enough experience – only 6 months in a company that I have never heard of. She does speak Afrikaans and Dutch, though, which would be good if we used her in our branch in Holland. She's only 21. Her telephone number is 0210 345876 (not the same as the one on the application form).

Task

Use the information above to complete the table below.

CANDIDATES' DETAILS

(Complete in capitals)

1 Name: Age: Length of experience: Contact details: Languages:	2 Name: Age: Length of experience: Contact details: Languages:
3 Name: Age: Length of experience: Contact details: Languages:	4 Name: Age: Length of experience: Contact details: Languages:

(20 marks)

LCCI TEST 2

Further practice and guidance

Question 1

Exercise 1

What sort of style and writing do you think is required here? Would it be better to write long and complicated sentences full of details, or do you think it would be better to give all the necessary points clearly and concisely?

Can you give an example of a long sentence telling the time, date and place of the training, and then think of a shorter way of giving the same information?

_____

_____

Exercise 2

Notice the reason for the training day: for customer relations. This suggests that this memo would also try to be positive towards its target readers (that is, the people invited to the training day). Can you think of any positive language or facts which might make the staff feel happy about working on a Saturday, as the question says they have to?

_____

_____

Exercise 3

Set out the first point of the task simply, perhaps thinking of the person who is going to receive this information. The best way is to think of the subject – in this case it is information about the training day, so what do you think might be best as the 'subject heading' (title)?

_____

Exercise 4

Let's look at some spelling problems or vocabulary problems which might come up in this letter.

a) You are writing to people you work with. What are these people called? Clue: this word begins with 'c'.

   _____

b) Give a word which means very short. Clue: it is used in the question you have been given.

   _____

c) Give a word which means that you must do something. Clue: it is a long word which is used in the question which you have been given.

   _____

d) Can you give a word which means the opposite of the previous word? Clue: this word begins with 'v'.

   _____

Check the spellings of these words very carefully.

Exercise 5

Why do you think that the training might be needed?

_____

If you were attending this training, what would you like to see included in the day? (Perhaps use your experience if you have attended a day like this one). You don't have to include this in the memo, but it might help to imagine yourself in this situation to make it sound more authentic.

Don't forget to think what kind of customers they may be – imagine the reader of your letter in your head and this will help you to be more focused and clear in what you say in the memo.

Exercise 6

Look at these two possible answers to Question 1, only one of which is appropriate. Look at them both and think about the style, the grammar and the vocabulary.

In both memos:

a)   underline the information you need for the training day

b)   underline any short forms (contractions)

c)   underline any spelling mistakes (there are three to find).

Model Answer A

MEMORANDUM

TO: Everyone!

FROM: Me

DATE: Today

SUBJECT: Training

Hi everyone!

Well, it's that time of year again – the training day for us all. It'll be on Sat 26 Sept all day.

You know the company thinks it's good with its costumers and always wants to tell everyone what to do, especially as some newpapers say we're rubbish.

'Cos of that everyone must come on Saturday. Tell someone if you can't make it.

We'll meet in the usuaul place, and you'll also get things given to you. We'll work together too, so it shouldn't be too much hard work.

The day will start at 1000 and will go on for the whole day, but there will be some kind of lunch.

Sorry about all this, but there you are!

See you soon!

Model Answer B

MEMORANDUM

TO: All colleagues – Complaints Dept

FROM: A Smith – HR

DATE: 21. 08. 09

SUBJECT: Training Day

Please note that the next training day for ALL members of the Complaints Department will take place on Saturday 26 September from 1000 – 1630.

As you are aware, the company prides itself on good customer relations, and tries to hold a training day every year to keep our valued staff updated with the latest techniques. During the past year, however, the company has received some rather bad publicity in the newspapers regarding the confused and slow handling of customer complaints.

Because of this, we have no alternative but to make the training COMPULSORY for all colleagues. Please contact your line manager if you have any problems with this.

The training will be held in the Conference Centre. On arrival, please report to Reception, where you will be given a badge and materials for use during the day, as well as information telling you which group you have been allocated to.

The introductory talk at 1030 will be in Macmillan Hall, then small group workshops will take place until lunch, which will be at 1300 in the main restaurant. After lunch, workshops will resume and the final session will again be in the Macmillan Hall at 1600.

Exercise 7

Decide which one is more suitable for the answer to the question you have been given. Is all the information given in both answers?

Question 2

Although this text and questions are about a bank, the information is more concerned with the company itself, than about money.

Exercise 8

What information do we learn about the following?

a) the bank's plans

---

b) its existing customers

---

c) the bank's policy

---

d) the number of branches

Exercise 9

What is the tone of the text? Is it formal with lots of facts and figures or is it more informative and friendly? What it the effect of using 'we' and 'our' frequently in the text? Write some words/phrases which give a feeling of the tone.

_____

_____

Exercise 10

There are some words in the text which could have more than one meaning depending on the context. What are they?

a) One word also means 'a noise'.   _____

b) One word also means 'parts of a tree'.   _____

c) One word means 'something you can wear on your finger'. _____

Exercise 11

Find at least three amounts of money which are mentioned in the text. What are they? Clue: look for the number first and then see what the number refers to.

_____

_____

_____

Exercise 12

Can you find any vocabulary in this text which it would be a good idea to make a note of for future use? For example, try and find the following words and phrases in the article – you are given the definition, but you must find the word.

a) what people think of your company   _____

b) cut down (on)   _____

c) you are this when you use the services of a company   _____

d) activity on your account   _____

e) very large   _____

f) encourage somebody to do something   _____

g) the most modern   _____

h) business gathering   _____

Question 3

Exercise 13

How many different things can a computer be used for? Write at least five.

_____

_____

_____

_____

_____

Vocabulary: | *computers* |

Exercise 14

Look at the verbs and nouns in the two columns. Match them together to make phrases to do with using computers.

a) surf   a file

b) click   the internet

c) download   up or down

d) scroll   music

e) save   in or out

f) log   the mouse

Exercise 15

Use the phrases above to complete the following sentences. Make changes where necessary.

a) To check your email, you have to _____ .

b) I save loads of money by _____ from the internet. (Clue: change the verb form).

c) Make sure you _____ your _____ before shutting down the computer.

d) I really should stop _____ and start studying! (Clue: change the verb form).

e) If you can't see the whole screen, you can _____ .

f) _____ on the file you want to open.

Exercise 16

Look carefully at the material which is about specifications for the computers. Remember that you do not have to be a computer expert – you are comparing facts and figures.

Highlight the words in the boxes which show the reader that the material is about computers.

Exercise 17

Notice how the information is given quite briefly, with each product in its own separate box. Are there boxes which seem to be longer in their content?

_____

Exercise 18

Are there any boxes which have some information which is exactly the same?

_____

Exercise 19

What do the following numbers refer to?

a) 322.96 _____   b) 160 _____

c) 503 _____   d) 17 _____

e) 1 _____

Exercise 20

Look at the questions you have to answer. Give two examples of each of the following:

a) questions where you have to compare the information   _____

b) questions where you have to find something different about the computer   _____

c) questions where you have to give a number.   _____

Exercise 21

These words have been spelt backwards. What are they? You will find them all in the boxes.

a) yromem _____   b) enohp   _____

c) yreviled _____   d) neercsediw   _____

e) detimil _____

Question 4

This exercise contains plenty of information about the candidates interviewed for a job, but do not let all the details distract you. Look carefully at the boxes which you have to fill in, and also note the numbering. Remember that the details you have to find may not be in the same order as in the texts.

Exercise 22

How many pieces of information do you have to find about each person? How many answers will require numbers?

_____

Exercise 23

Look at the headings for the Candidates' Details (name etc.). What questions were the candidates asked to get this information?

_____

_____

_____

_____

_____

Exercise 24

Write questions to find out information about the following things, then test them on your partner or a friend if possible.

a) Interests and hobbies   b) Ambitions   c) Travel abroad   d) Education

_____

_____

_____

_____

Exercise 25

In each paragraph, what is the first RELEVANT piece of information you are given?

Paragraph 1 _____

Paragraph 2 _____

Paragraph 3 _____

Paragraph 4 _____

Exercise 26

Which candidate does NOT give a phone number for contact?

_____

Exercise 27

How many candidates are under 35? What are their names?

_____

Exercise 28

Which candidate speaks more than two languages?

_____

Exercise 29

Can you find some positive words and phrases which are used about the candidates?

_____

Exercise 30

Can you find some negative words and phrases which are used about the candidates?

_____

Exercise 31

Can you think of any more positive or negative words that could be used about someone?

Look at the definitions which follow and see if you can work out the words. You are given the first letter of each word to help you.

Positive

tidily dressed = s_____

having everything ready = o_____

having suitable training = q_____

Negative

untidily dressed = s_____

not arriving on time = u_____

making mistakes = c_____

Exercise 32

Which candidate do you think will be employed?

_____

Exercise 33

The information given to you is written in note form. How do we make notes? For example, what kinds of words are missing? Look in the following sentences.

a) the first sentence about the first candidate   _____

b) all of the sentences about the third candidate   _____

c) the second and third sentences about the fourth candidate.   _____

Exercise 34

Look at these sentences and make short notes by leaving out 'unnecessary' words.

a) Mrs Green rang to ask if she could meet you at 6pm.

_____

b) Please can you find out the availability of product number 10136 quickly.

_____

c) The office will be closed from 1-2pm every day for lunch.

_____

d) Please can you ring Mr Cox today after 4pm on telephone number 03477 870654.

_____

Exercise 35

Look at this short text and note down five important facts. How many words did you use?

Mr Wales rang us today from our Rome office. He said it was very important that he speaks to you personally about our recent sales figures, which are very bad. He is available until 8pm tonight. Please could you phone him to discuss this matter which employees are very worried about.

(50 words)

_____

_____

_____

_____

LCCI TEST 3

PAPER 1 READING AND WRITING 2 hours

QUESTION 1

Situation

You are a recently employed Sales Executive responsible for the launch of new products by your company – Express Printing plc.

Task

Write a letter of between 150 and 200 words to existing customers informing them of a new printer which is about to come onto the market. Include the following:

- your name and direct line telephone number
- information about a product discount for a short time
- a statement about the improved efficiency of the new product
- an offer of free, fast delivery for a limited period only.

Remember that you have been taken on by Express Printing plc to increase their sales, which have been falling recently.

Write your **letter** in the space below.

(30 marks)

QUESTION 2

Situation

You work for a popular car magazine. This month you have an exclusive story about a new 'hybrid' car which is just coming onto the market.

Task

Read the article below entitled " 'PLUG-IN' HYBRID ARRIVES", then say whether the statements on the next page are **TRUE or FALSE.** Then **quote** the words or phrases from the article that support your answer. Do **not** write more than 6 supporting words for each answer. You will lose marks if you write more than this.

Note: Answers are usually in 2 parts. You may need to look in different places in the article to find the supporting words you need.

Example:

Statement: There is going to be a Motorcycle Show in Oldtown Arena.

Answer: FALSE   International Car Show/Newtown Arena

'PLUG-IN' HYBRID ARRIVES

At last, some bright news in the otherwise somewhat gloomy picture which is the background to next week's International Car Show in Newtown Arena.

A fairly unknown Asian car manufacturer has come up with the world's first 'plug-in' hybrid car, ahead of all those other car companies which have been fighting to do just the same thing – and it will be presented for the first time later this month, at Newtown!

The company, which has only recently joined the car development arena, is one of the biggest producers of batteries for laptops and computers, and it is believed that a well-known Russian tycoon has already invested heavily in the company.

The car, as yet unnamed, is a small 4-door vehicle, with an electric motor and a 1-litre petrol engine. The car can be powered by either method.

If the battery is fully charged, the car can travel about 85 kilometres. The petrol engine can then take over, and even recharge the batteries. But the design intention is that the car will be charged overnight from the normal domestic electricity mains.

The car will be sold within a year for about £15,000, in a number of small cities near its development site, and hopefully it will be on sale worldwide at a similar price within 3 years.

The secret of the car will be revealed at the show, but technical experts think that the company has capitalized on its expertise with batteries, adapting its products for use in the car. It is the composition of the battery which has held up the larger manufacturers, alongside concerns over safety and reliability.

This new product will not put a smile on the faces of some of the big international car manufacturers attending the event. They are already facing severe economic problems, which in turn could affect labour markets in a number of countries.

Write your answers on the lines marked A.

1   Car manufacturers are in an unhappy situation and facing a great deal of financial pressure.

A   _____

2   The new 'plug-in' hybrid is made by a computer manufacturer; it has a Russian designer.

A   _____

3   The car has two recharging methods.

A   _____

4   The car will be sold worldwide this year, after 3 years of development.

A   _____

5   The car's name will be revealed at the show; it uses a computer battery.

A   _____

6   The car will sell globally for about £15,000.

A   _____

7   Other attempts to produce a 'plug-in' hybrid have been delayed due to worries over safety.

A   _____

8   Some big overseas companies are attending the vehicle exhibition soon.

A   _____

9   The car's design probably depends on the make-up of its battery.

A   _____

10 Some big car manufacturers are facing major difficulties which could cause unemployment.

A   _____

(30 marks)

QUESTION 3

Situation

You work in a local office. This week you will be preparing a report for your boss about some new equipment the office needs. You have to make sure you can answer all of his questions.

Task

Study the information in the advertisement below, then answer the questions which follow. **Write your answer as a single word, a name or a figure in the answer column.**

OFFICE SUPPLIES INC.
SPRING SALE!

EXECUTIVE LOW-BACK LEATHER CHAIR
Ref. 397858
Available in black or brown
Special price £29
Save £10!

2-DRAWER MOBILE FILING CABINET
Ref. 397772
Available in blue, red or white
Special price £29
Save £15 on original price!

Half-price offers
COMPUTER KEYBOARD 3000
Ref. 395065
Now £24.50
Previously £49!

KASKI'S SECURITY PROGRAM
Ref. 396124
Now £20
Previously £40!

We have over 5,000 products in stock.
Special discounts available for larger orders (5%)
Come and see us TODAY!
Open 7 days a week from 8 am to 8 pm.
Telephone 0800 0221133 any time.

ANSWERS

1   How many products can you buy from Office Supplies Inc.?

2   Which product is available in red?

3   Which product has a saving of £10?

4   Which product used to cost £49?

5   In how many colours is the chair?

6   Give the reference number of the security programme.

7   What time does the company close?

8   How many products are half-price?

9   What is the name of the security programme?

10   What is the benefit of larger orders?

11   Which product uses the number 3,000?

12   What is the saving on a low-back chair?

13   What is the telephone number of the company?

14   What are the chairs made of?

15   When is the best time to telephone Office Supplies Inc.?

16   How much discount is offered?

17   Which product has the reference number 397772?

18   How many days a week is Office Supplies Inc. open?

19   How many drawers does the filing cabinet have?

20   How much do you save on the filing cabinet?

(20 marks)

QUESTION 4

Situation

You work for a large distribution company which has a number of branches abroad. As part of a training programme, some managers are coming to visit the UK plant. Your boss wants you to plan the week's visits and has left you these notes.

1) Mr Choi will be visiting us on Wednesday 16th. Please make sure that you meet him in Reception at 1000 and arrange lunch for him at 1300. Don't forget that he will require a vegetarian meal! He will be taken to the main sorting area at 1130, where he will be guided around the site by Ms Wells. Please make sure that he leaves by 1630, as he has another appointment in London in the evening.

2) Also on Wednesday, we have two other visitors. Mr Smith is coming to see me, so I will make all the arrangements, but his colleague is being looked after by Mr Jenkins. Please make sure that lunch is arranged for Mr Allsop at 1330. Mr Allsop is coming to see the Human Resources Department. When he has finished there, please bring him to my office for a short meeting. Mr Allsop and his colleague will arrive at about 1215.

3) Mr Svensson is coming for a tour of the Mailing Department on Monday. He'll be here all day, so please make sure that coffee is available on his arrival at 1030. He doesn't require lunch here, as I will be taking him into town for a working lunch. I hope Ms Wells will be available to guide him around, but please check with her. If she isn't available, please let me know immediately.

4) Mr Coombs will be meeting Mr Andersson at Reception on Thursday. Mr Andersson is here to see the Data Room and to hold some discussions about closer co-operation. Please organize a light lunch for him at 1230, which should give him time to talk to some of our key workers before he leaves to catch his flight at 1800. He will be here quite early, about 0900. You'll need to make sure everything is ready, as he'll have a busy day ahead of him.

Task

Use the information above to complete the table below.

TIMETABLE OF VISITS

(Complete in capitals)

NAME	DATE OF VISIT	ARRIVAL TIME	LUNCH DETAILS	IN CHARGE OF VISIT
1				
2				
3				
4				

(20 marks)

QUESTION 1

Exercise 1

Look carefully at who you are in this task, and look at your role in this company. What kind of person do you think would be employed, and what kind of language would you use when you contact customers? For example, would you be very formal and just give facts, or would you want to sound more enthusiastic in order to encourage your customers to read the information and contact you?

Exercise 2

Think of some positive words to describe a product which you frequently use – your MP3 player / mobile phone / satellite navigation system – and try to use them in your letter. For example, I have a touch phone, which I might describe like this:

'It's really useful, fast and efficient, as well as smart and state-of-the-art technology.'

Exercise 3

Can you think of any negative words about new technology? See if you can complete the words given below. Be careful – all the vowel letters (AEIOU) are missing.

a) -xp-ns-v- _____   b) -nr-l- - bl- _____

c) c-mp-t-r cr-sh (2 words) _____   d) c-mpl-c-t-d _____

Exercise 4

Look carefully at all the points you have to include in your letter. Be specific and give 'real' names and numbers and don't just lift phrases from the question. Check when you have finished your letter that you have included everything you were asked to do. How many points do you have to include in this letter?

Exercise 5

Can you think of useful phrases which could be helpful in your letter? Find words or phrases which mean the following in the model answer on the following page.

a) there is no cost _____

b) the product will not break down so often _____

c) you can get the product quickly _____

d) respected name _____

e) quite a long time _____

f) someone the company knows well _____

g) (most) modern (product) _____

Question 1

Model Answer

Express Printing plc Wolverstock Road Sussex S19 8HT

18th September 2009

Products Manager
Merchant Printers
Greene's Industrial Estate
Birmingham BE9 6ME

Dear Customer,

I am pleased to introduce myself to you. My name is *(Mary Porter)* and I have recently joined Express Printing plc, where I am looking forward to working with you.

I have worked for a number of years in Sales, but Express Printing has such a good reputation for the high standard of its products that I cannot think of a better place to work.

I would like to introduce Express Printing's latest product – the XXON printer/photocopier, which is released this month. This printer is one of the fastest of its generation, with the new feature of remote control, and improved reliability.

As an already-valued customer, we would like to offer you the chance to see and use this product for yourself. We offer you the super-efficient XXON printer with 20% off and immediate delivery. Both offers are only available this month.

In addition, we would like to include 6 months' service and installation – all at no charge.

Please contact me on my direct line *(0172 911108)* to take advantage of this offer, and feel free to pass this information on to any of your clients who may also be interested in our company.

I hope to hear from you soon.

Yours sincerely,

(Mary Porter)

Sales Executive

(190 words)

Exercise 6

Look at this extract from another letter and see if you can fill in the missing words, which are useful phrases which you have already had in this book. You have been given the first letter of each word to help you.

The meeting, which is c_____ for all members of staff, will take place on Monday 21 August. We wish to improve relations with our a_____ -v_____ c_____ and r_____ some recent problems which have happened.

Please c_____ that you can attend the meeting, and do not h_____ to c_____ me if there are any problems.

> **Tip!**
>
> Remember to include a date and the two addresses in your letter: your company's address and the address of the person you are writing to.

Question 2

Most people are interested in cars, and this is about a new type of car which is also friendly to the environment.

Exercise 7

Scan the text to find words or phrases which are positive or negative about the car market at the moment.

_____

_____

Exercise 8

Find three places or nationalities which are mentioned in the text. What do they have to do with cars and the information given?

_____

_____

_____

Exercise 9

Find four numbers in the text. What do they refer to? Remember to note the paragraph number.

_____

_____

_____

_____

Exercise 10

Read the definitions below and find the words in the text. Highlight them and note their paragraph number.

a) a combination (clue: more than one thing)   _____

b) a lot (clue: weight)   _____

c) completely (clue: everything)   _____

d) shown (clue: you can see this)   _____

e) used well (clue: a word often used with money)   _____

Exercise 11

Highlight as many words as you can relating to cars in the text.

Exercise 12

This 'hybrid' car is still very new and it is going to bring some 'bright news' now and in the future to the car market. We do not know the exact date when the car was first developed, but that is not really important. We know it was **before** this article was written and before the International Car Show. We know the idea **is** exciting and we know that the car may have an effect on the **future**.

Can you find any verb forms in paragraphs 2, 3, and 7 which connect **before, now** and possibly the **future** together? Clue: this verb form is called the present perfect.

_____

Exercise 13

We often use this verb form when the definite or exact time is not so important, or it is clear when we are speaking about from the context. Can you think of any words which are often used with this form? Clue: two of them are in paragraph 3.

Grammar: | *tenses* |

Exercise 14

Look at the table which gives some basic information about tenses.

Tense	Example	Use
Present simple	I work in an office.	This shows an activity which I do every day or regularly.
Present continuous	She is writing a report.	This is an activity which she is doing at the moment of speaking, or a temporary action around the present time.
Past simple	I worked in an office.	This is an activity which I did before, but not any longer. There is often a time phrase with a sentence like this e.g. *last year*, *last month*.
Past continuous	They were writing a report when the phone rang.	This often shows an activity which was happening when another activity happened.
Present perfect simple	He has worked in an office.	This shows that the person has worked in an office, but we do not know when – we know only that it is 'before now'.

Write full sentences using the prompts below, putting the verbs in the correct tenses. Add any extra words if necessary. What tense is used in each sentence?

a) He/travel/work/bus/every day

---

b) The Department/work/efficiently/last month

---

c) The boss/have/meeting/during his lunch break

---

d) She/visit/office/Rome/at the moment

---

e) The company/sell/lots of televisions/this year

Question 3

Notice with this question you are given extra information, as well as the product information, so it is really important to look at everything on the page. Remember to look at the questions first, so that you have a good idea what you are looking for when you look at all the information you are given.

Exercise 15

How many questions are normally in this section? How many separate products or pieces of product information are usually given?

Exercise 16

Look at the questions given and find how many begin with the different question words: *how many/much, which, what, why, when*. What kind of information does each question word want?

Exercise 17

Which answer, 1 or 2, is an appropriate response to the questions below?

Question	*Possible answers*
a) How many employees are there?	1) 60
	2) They are all well-trained.
b) How much information do you need?	1) As much as possible.
	2) I need five.
c) Which report is the most important?	1) It's a very interesting report.
	2) The one written in January.
d) What's the HR Manager's name?	1) William Wood
	2) His office is on the second floor.
e) Why are you so late?	1) The train was delayed.
	2) I always catch the train.
f) When do you need the report?	1) Next week, please.
	2) Because we need to read it now.

Exercise 18

How many figures can you find in the questions? This probably means you will need to give a word or a name in the answer, rather than another number.

Exercise 19

Notice that the information is on two sides of the page. What is different about the details on the right-hand side of the page?

Exercise 20

Which two products have colours mentioned?

Exercise 21

Office vocabulary is useful to know. See if you can find items of office equipment and furniture in this puzzle. There are six words to find: three are vertical and three are horizontal.

e	g	i	k	l	m	f	x	x	a	y	q	p	s
f	h	y	l	k	l	f	i	c	z	n	p	q	a
f	h	y	l	k	l	i	i	c	z	n	p	q	a
w	p	o	f	u	b	l	z	p	y	v	m	z	s
c	o	m	p	u	t	e	r	d	d	e	f	x	m
m	o	o	c	w	t	k	g	b	n	m	x	p	p
m	u	u	a	d	p	r	e	k	l	c	s	w	i
m	o	s	b	c	d	s	e	h	t	p	l	n	v
b	k	e	y	b	o	a	r	d	g	f	s	e	n
v	d	h	e	d	a	n	l	e	c	d	s	l	k
v	j	f	j	t	c	z	x	s	c	r	e	e	n
d	j	o	p	b	c	x	m	k	g	f	s	k	m

Question 4

Remember that the material you are asked to find is not always given in the same order as the table you have to fill in, so highlight or underline the relevant information. You could also note where you are going to use it, for example put 'N' for name or 'D' for date.

Exercise 22

Skim each paragraph and find the days which are mentioned in each of them. Highlight them.

Exercise 23

What times are referred to on Wednesday 16th; Monday; Thursday? Look at these three days, and see if there are any times connected with them – what are they? Note: there may be more than one time mentioned on each day.

_____

_____

_____

Exercise 24

a) In each paragraph, there are at least two people mentioned. Who are they?

Paragraph	Person 1	Person 2	Person 3
1			
2			
3			
4			

b) Which person do you NOT have to make arrangements for? _____

Exercise 25

Look at these clues, and find the words in each paragraph.

a) Paragraph 1: a meal without meat, fish or eggs   _____

                 a formal word meaning 'meeting'   _____

b) Paragraph 2: a formal word for 'plans'   _____

c) Paragraph 3: this word is used three times! Give the negative form.   _____

d) Paragraph 4: a word which means 'working together'   _____

Exercise 26

Use the text to answer these questions.

a) Paragraph 1: Which verb usually goes with 'appointment'?

     _____

b) Paragraph 2: Which verb usually goes with 'arrangements'?

     _____

c) Paragraph 4: What word has a similar meaning to 'arrange'?

     _____

Exercise 27

Look at these useful phrases which you could use in letters or reports.

place an order	promote a product	do business with
confirm a (hotel/flight) reservation	leave a message	

Using these phrases, rewrite the sentences below. Make changes where necessary.

a) I would like to tell you I am definitely flying to Stockholm tomorrow.

_____

b) The company wants to make people buy its new sales item all over the world.

_____

c) Our company works with other international companies.

_____

d) 'Sorry, he's not at his desk at the moment. You can tell me what you want to say to him.'

_____

e) 'We would like to arrange for you to send us your materials.'

_____

Grammar: | *prefixes* |

Exercise 28

Exercise 25 asked you to give a negative form of a word. We can often make positive adjectives negative by adding something to the beginning of the word. This is called a prefix.

Look at these prefixes and match them to the adjectives to make negative adjectives. You will have to use some more than once.

| un   im   dis   il   mis   in |

a) possible   _____

b) satisfactory   _____

c) legal   _____

d) polite   _____

e) continued   _____

f) lucky   _____

g) visible   _____

h) understand   _____

Exercise 29

Using the negative adjectives above, complete these sentences.

a) Your work has been very _____ this month and you must work harder.

b) If you do something _____ , you could go to prison.

c) You can't buy this particular sort of printer any more, it's been _____.

d) If you _____ the instructions in the test, you might fail.

e) John didn't get the job because he was _____ to the interviewer.

f) It's _____ to travel from London to Edinburgh in a day for a business meeting!

g) She was very _____ and got stuck in traffic for over an hour.

h) The road sign was _____ in the rain so we didn't turn left and got lost.

LCCI TEST 4

PAPER 1 READING AND WRITING 2 hours

QUESTION 1

Situation

You work in the Customer Relations Department of J L P Computing Services.

You have recently received a number of complaints from both individual and business customers. These complaints concern a special program which your company has installed on computers also supplied by you.

Task

Write a letter of between 150 and 200 words to these customers including the following:

- an apology for the inconvenience caused
- a brief explanation of the problem
- the action to be taken by your company (such as the replacement of equipment or compensation)
- information about what customers should do (including contact names and telephone numbers for your company)
- a reassurance for the future.

Write your **letter** in the space below.

(30 marks)

QUESTION 2

Situation

You work for a large insurance company where you are training some new employees to explain policies to new customers.

Task

Read the text below entitled "DEALING WITH CUSTOMERS", then say whether the statements which follow are **TRUE or FALSE.** Then **quote** the words or phrases from the text that support your answer. Do **not** write more than 6 supporting words for each answer. You will lose marks if you write more than this.

Note: Answers are usually in 2 parts. You may need to look in different places in the text to find the supporting words you need.

Example:

Statement: Customers need to understand what their insurance covers; staff should try to be clear and helpful.

Answer: TRUE   important/be careful to explain clearly

DEALING WITH CUSTOMERS

1 It is very important that the customer understands the type of insurance he or she has bought. Be very careful to explain terms clearly – for example, when '**we**' is used, this means *our* insurance company, not you and the customer! In the same way, '**you**' refers to the customer and any member of his or her family living with him or her.

2 Make sure the customer knows that we have arranged a number of useful services which are available 24 hours a day, every day of the year. For example, we have a service called **Home Emergency**, which will arrange for help or repairs to the home if there is storm damage, water damage due to leaks in a central heating system, or damage caused by drainage problems.

3 A particularly useful optional service which is often forgotten by the customer, but which is also always available, is the **Advice Line on Legal Matters**. It offers confidential advice on any personal legal subject (although calls are recorded for security purposes). Remind customers, however, that this is a service which they must purchase when they buy their insurance.

4 To help customers and ourselves, always advise them to **check their policy** before they make a claim, to make sure that the loss or damage is covered under the policy.

5 By the way, customers should have all the relevant telephone numbers supplied to them in our special **QuickPack**, which gives all the contact information needed at a glance.

Check they have received this essential advice.

6 Two important areas which must not be overlooked are the customer's **right to cancel**, and how the customer should complain, if necessary. Policyholders may cancel their policies if all documents received from us are returned within 14 days. **Complaints** can be raised by customers in a number of ways: by telephoning our special complaints hotline; by talking to the person dealing with their claim; or in writing. Again, all the relevant contact details are in the QuickPack. Remind the customers of this.

Write your answers on the lines marked A.

1   Staff should tell the customer what their policy means; customers should refer to their policy before making a claim.

A   ——

2   Home Emergency is the only service available, and the insurers arrange for repairs only.

A   ——

3   Legal advice is free, but can be used only when a policy is bought.

A   ——

4   The legal advice is not private; it is recorded and anyone can listen to it.

A   ——

5   QuickPack is easy to use and has important information in it.

A   ——

6   All customers can cancel, but there is a time limit.

A   ——

7   Home Emergency can't organize help or repairs to the home if there is a type of damage caused by the weather.

A   ——

8   The customer's right to cancel is not important and not all the relevant contact details are in the QuickPack.

A   ——

9   The Advice Line on Legal Matters is compulsory, and doesn't have to be bought when customers buy their insurance.

A   ——

10 There are several ways to complain, for instance by letter.

A   ——

(30 marks)

QUESTION 3

Situation

You work for a consumer organization which checks the best prices of products. This week you are looking at energy in the home, and comparing the prices of 4 large companies.

Task

Study the information in the table below, then answer the questions which follow. **Write your answer as a single word, a name or a figure in the answer column.**

Company:	GASLINE	Plan: Click 6 (online) Pay: monthly
Cancellation:	Any time (no penalty) with 1 month's notice	
Comments:	Cost can change £1,057 a year (3-bedroom house) Bills online only	

Company:	ALLPOWER	Plan: Fixed Energy Pay: every 3 months
Cancellation:	£25 - electricity (cancel before end of year) £15 - gas (cancel before end of year) No cancellation fee if moving	
Comments:	Fixed price £1,213 p.a. No benefit to customer if prices go down	

Company:	BEACON ELECTRIC	Plan: Energy Plus Pay: monthly
Cancellation:	£20	
Comments:	Cost fixed for first year; then can change £1,200 a year Paper or online bills	

Company:	EXPRESS	Plan: CostLess Pay: monthly or every 3 months
Cancellation:	No penalty with 2 months' notice (otherwise 1-month penalty)	
Comments:	Fixed price for 18 months £1,150 a year (3-bedroom house) Discount if bills are paid online	

ANSWERS

1   Which company's plan is called Energy Plus?

2   How much must I pay if I want to cancel Allpower gas this year?

3   Which company charges a £20 cancellation fee?

4   Which company wants payment every 3 months?

5   What is the name of the company which prefers users to use computers?

6   How much is the cancellation fee with Beacon Electric?

7   Which company's prices do not change for the first 12 months?

8   Whose price is the lowest, for one year?

9   How can you get your bills from Beacon Electric?

10   How much is Gasline's cancellation charge?

11   Which companies have prices that do not change?

12   Which company does not change a cancellation fee if you move house?

13   Which supplier has a 12-month, fixed-price contract?

14   What is the name of Express's energy plan?

15   Which companies might be most reasonable if prices go down?

16   Which company has different prices for the cancellation of gas and electricity?

17   What is the difference in notice periods between Gasline and Express?

18   Which company lets customers choose how they pay?

19   What is the cancellation fee you might have to pay with Express?

20   Why is it best to use a computer to pay Express's bills?

(20 marks)

QUESTION 4

Situation

You are the Director of a large IT company. Next week you are visiting a large exhibition in Los Angeles. Your PA has left you these messages.

---

1 On Monday you will attend the opening of the Exhibition at 1800. This will be followed by a reception in the Metropolitan Hotel, where you will meet their representative, John Smith. Solutions are sponsoring these opening events, by the way.

2 You will be meeting Mr Jameson of Sjoden's on Tuesday. He will pick you up from your hotel at 1015, and take you to his offices on Denver Street. His phone number is 0044 5621078. Don't forget to congratulate him on his son's forthcoming marriage, will you?

3 On Thursday you are visiting NewIdeasUSA.com at their offices in San Francisco. Transport has been arranged for you, and they will meet you at 1300. Details will be confirmed by email to your hotel, once you are in Los Angeles. I think you already know their representative, Ms Livingston, who is going to be in charge of your visit there.

4 Friday will be an early start – you have a working breakfast with Mr Fellows at his hotel, the Elvet, on Dartington Square. A taxi will pick you up at 0830, so you should have plenty of time. He will phone you on Thursday evening to finalize a programme for the meeting. The rest of the day will be spent taking a final look at the exhibition stands, before you head to the airport for your overnight flight back to the UK.

Task

Use the information above to complete the schedule below.

LOS ANGELES EXHIBITION SCHEDULE

(Complete in capitals)

COMPANY	DAY AND TIME	CONTACT PERSON	CONTACT DETAILS	YOUR DESTINATION
1				
2				
3				
4				

(20 marks)

LCCI TEST 4

Question 1

Exercise 1

How many ways can you think of saying sorry? Complete the phrases below.

a) S_____y!

b) I am v_____ s_____.

c) We must a_____ for these problems.

d) We r_____ this mistake.

e) We r_____ the in_____ caused.

Try and use some of these phrases in your letter of apology.

Exercise 2

Match these phrases for starting and ending a letter together. What kind of letters are they: to a customer, a friend, or your new bank?

a) Dear Sir   See you soon   _____

b) Dear Fred   Yours sincerely   _____

c) Dear Mr Smith   Yours faithfully   _____

Notice the spelling and the use of capital letters in the phrases 'Yours faithfully' and 'Yours sincerely'. Be careful how you start and finish your letter.

Exercise 3

All the following words, with the letters NOT in the correct order, are words to do with things companies sell. Can you work them out?

a) oodgs _____   b) ouprdcts _____   c) emsti _____

d) emctpsruo _____   e) magrrop _____   f) rtnrpei _____

These words may be useful in your letter.

Exercise 4

These are the definitions. What are the words? You have been given the first letter of each word.

a) could not be helped u_____   b) money returned to you r_____

c) period of waiting d_____

Vocabulary: | *British and American spelling* |

If you look back at Exercise 1, and check your answer for 1c, you will see that there are two ways of spelling this word. Both are correct and equally acceptable, but you must be consistent in your work. With an 's', it is British English, and with a 'z' it is American English.

Exercise 5

Look at these words. Try and decide which words are spelt the British way, and which words are spelt the American way. Write 'Am' or 'Br' next to each word.

a) realize ___   b) realise ___   c) color ___   d) colour ___

e) centre ___   f) center ___   g) tire ___   h) tyre ___

i) cheque ___   j) check ___   k) catalog ___   l) catalogue ___

Some words are also different in American English. For example, in the UK the word 'rubbish' is used, while in the USA the word would be 'garbage'.

Exercise 6

Here are some American words. Do you know which word would probably be used in the UK? Again, remember that both are equally correct. Use your dictionary if you need to.

American English	British English
sidewalk	
gas/gasoline	
elevator	
fall (part of the year)	
to stand in line	
subway	

Exercise 7

Look at this extract from a model answer to a complaint. Can you find any American words or phrases in it? Clue: there are seven words or phrases. Do you know the British way of spelling the word or the British word? Remember both ways are equally acceptable.

> We are sorry to hear there is a problem with our hire truck. Please call us on area code 008899 883397 with call collect so that we can talk about this. Our office is open Monday through Friday.
>
> We also enclose a color catalog of our other trucks, some with automatic gear shift.

American words/phrases: _____ _____ _____

_____ _____ _____ _____

British words/phrases: _____ _____ _____

_____ _____ _____ _____

Exercise 8

Look at this next extract from another model answer. Some words are missing. Can you replace them? You are given the first letter of each word.

> Thank you for your r_____ email. We are disappointed to hear that you are d_____ with our product.
>
> We would like the opportunity to discuss this with you. Please c_____ our office at your earliest c_____ to arrange an a_____ with our Sales Manager, who will be pleased to meet you.

Exercise 9

Read the complete model answer below and highlight and make notes of any vocabulary and phrases that you can use in your own letter writing.

Question 1

Model Answer

J L P Computing Services Station Road Harlow Essex SS20 3AB

27th July 2009

IT Manager
A.T.T. Insurance
Westgate
York Y50 1DD

Dear Customer,

Thank you for your recent letter. We are very sorry to hear that you have been experiencing some problems with our latest software package.

Unfortunately, it would appear that there is a problem with the program, which we are working hard to solve.

We would like to take this opportunity to apologize for any inconvenience caused, and we will send a service engineer to you, at your convenience, to reinstall the program and, if necessary, replace the computer itself.

Additionally, we would like to offer you 1 year's free servicing on all equipment already supplied by us to you, and a 10% discount on your next order.

Please contact me on my direct line (0932 876890) or email (p.barker@jlpcomps) to let me know a suitable time for us to visit your IT Department.

As a valued customer, we would like to reassure you that we do not take these problems lightly, and we will be taking further steps in quality control to ensure that such difficulties do not arise again.

Yours sincerely,

(Peter Barker)

Customer Relations

(173 words)

Question 2

Exercise 10

This is part of training information for insurance employees, so although the information is likely to be clear, it is also going to be quite 'compact', with a lot of points in quite a small space. It is very important that you read quickly and efficiently. Try to answer these questions as quickly as possible, by **skimming** and **scanning** the text.

How many paragraphs are there in the text? What is the first and last letter of each paragraph?

Exercise 11

How many times can you find the word 'insurance' and the word 'customer' in the text? Clue: one of these words is used in every paragraph, sometimes more than once.

_____

Exercise 12

There are a number of instructions given in the information. Can you find one in each paragraph?

Paragraph 1: _____

Paragraph 2: _____

Paragraph 3: _____

Paragraph 4: _____

Paragraph 5: _____

Paragraph 6: _____

Exercise 13

Looking at the previous question, can you summarize what the employees must do?

_____

Exercise 14

All the verb forms in the answers to exercise 12 are very direct, like a command or instruction. This is called the imperative form. Can you think of any words or phrases which you might use to make the command more polite? Clue: there is one word which begins with 'p' and there is a phrase with three words, but you must make some grammar changes.

_____

Grammar: | *the imperative* |

Exercise 15

Look at the information about forming the imperative, then write your own instructions based on the sentences below.

```
Imperative = bare infinitive of verb + object

Open (bare infinitive) the window. (object)

Hand in (bare infinitive) your report (object) by tomorrow morning.

Have (bare infinitive) a nice day! (object)
```

a) You want someone to complete a report by 5pm.

_____

b) You tell someone to visit a customer by the end of the week.

_____

c) You tell the staff to arrive on time in the mornings.

_____

d) You want your staff to install a new program on the computer.

_____

e) You want your secretary to arrange a flight to Copenhagen.

_____

Exercise 16

Look at the answers given for exercise 14, and use the phrase in front of each instruction from exercise 12. Make any necessary changes.

Paragraph 1: _____

Paragraph 2: _____

Paragraph 3: _____

Paragraph 4: _____

Paragraph 5: _____

Paragraph 6: _____

Exercise 17

What do these words and phrases mean in the numbered paragraphs? Look carefully at the context.

a) 2 emergency _____   b) 3 optional _____

c) 3 purchase _____   d) 5 relevant _____

e) 5 at a glance _____   f) 7 cancel _____

Exercise 18

Scan the text and see what services are available. Which is optional?

_____

Exercise 19

What does each service include?

_____

Question 3

This exercise contains a lot of material given in words rather than numbers, and with a lot of conditions applied to what you can do. You sometimes see this kind of material if you want to get a new mobile phone, for example, or a special travel card, and you have to look carefully to find which deal is going to be the best for you.

Exercise 20

What is the product that you are interested in here?

_____

Exercise 21

Look and find the names of the different companies and the kinds of plans they have. Highlight or underline all the information you find.

Exercise 22

The names of three of the companies will tell you something about their products which will help you with the questions. What is it?

_____

Exercise 23

Find the column that mentions 'Payment'. How often can you pay your bills with each company?

_____

Exercise 24

Scan the information again, and see if you can find these numbers. What are they? Each number has a clue to help you.

a) 1057 (cost for a year) _____

b) 6 (name of a plan) _____

c) 3 (number of something) _____

Exercise 25

Can you work out what these words are – the letters are in the wrong order. The first letter of each word is given to help you.

a) eanpytl p_____   b) aeaointllccn c_____

c) oiennl   o_____   d) ioutncsd   d_____

Exercise 26

Look at these definitions. Can you find the words? They are all in Test 4 Question 3.

a) Does not change   _____

b) Price cut   _____

c) A planned agreement will not take place _____

d) Payment for a service   _____

e) Advantage   _____

f) Punishment for breaking a contract   _____

g) Say in advance that you wish to end a contract _____

Question 4

Exercise 27

Scan the text and look at all the times in the different sections. Note them down and what happens at that time.

_____

_____

_____

_____

_____

Exercise 28

As we have been talking about time, let's revise the basic tenses again. Using the time clues in the sentences below, put the verbs in brackets into the correct tenses. Which tense is used in each sentence?

a) I (write) _____ the report this weekend.

Tense: _____

b) The company (make) _____ good profits recently.

Tense: _____

c) Prices (be) _____ lower last year.

Tense: _____

d) The boss (talk) _____ to the delegates when he was interrupted.

Tense: _____

e) My computer always (crash) _____ when I use this program.

Tense: _____

f) I can't answer the phone at the moment, I (have) _____ a meeting.

Tense: _____

Exercise 29

How many addresses can you find?

_____

Exercise 30

How many names of companies can you find? Are there also the names of people who work for them?

_____

Exercise 31

Are there any extra details in each paragraph which you do NOT need to fill in the table?

_____

Exercise 32

Can you find any examples of friendly and informal language in these notes? This might be short forms (contractions); extra phrases which are not really needed or words which are less formal.

_____

_____

Exercise 33

What would be a more formal way of writing the phrases you found in the previous question? Fill in the table.

Informal	Formal

Grammar: | *tag questions* |

Exercise 34

Look at the second message in Question 4, and notice the last sentence finishes 'will you?' This is called a 'tag phrase' and comes at the end of a tag question. Tag phrases are usually used to confirm what has already been said in an earlier part of the sentence, or to check whether something is true. They usually come at the end of a sentence in speech or in informal writing.

Look at these examples of tag questions. What do you notice about negatives and positives in these sentences?

It wasn't a very successful meeting, was it?

That's the new CEO, isn't it?

The customer didn't call back, did he?

You arrived late this morning, didn't you?

Remember that a tag phrase has a falling intonation when we speak, and when we are sure of the answer.

Exercise 35

Complete these tag questions with the correct phrases. The first letter of each is given to help you.

a) Business has improved, h_____?

b) The market is very slow today, i_____?

c) You don't like the new product, d_____?

d) The flight was very late, w_____?

e) The new boss will attend the meeting today, w_____?

Exercise 36

Unscramble the words below to do with air travel. The first letter of each is given to help you.

a) ivas v_____

b) ccekh ni c_____ i_____

c) sspptrao p_____

d) sstmcuo c_____

e) hcsudedel gthilf s_____ f_____

Candidate Answer Sheet

Mark your responses like this: ●
Do NOT mark your responses like this: ⊘ ⊗ ✓ ⊖ ○
Use an HB or No. 2 pencil only. Erase mistakes thoroughly.

Centre Code ☐☐☐☐☐☐

Test Number ☐☐☐☐☐☐

Candidate Name ☐☐☐☐☐☐☐☐☐☐☐☐☐☐☐☐☐☐☐☐☐☐☐☐

Exam Title ☐☐☐☐☐☐☐☐☐☐☐☐☐☐☐☐☐☐☐☐☐☐☐☐

CANDIDATE NUMBER

ORDER NUMBER

ANSWERS

1 Ⓐ Ⓑ Ⓒ Ⓓ	16 Ⓐ Ⓑ Ⓒ Ⓓ	31 Ⓐ Ⓑ Ⓒ Ⓓ	46 Ⓐ Ⓑ Ⓒ Ⓓ
2 Ⓐ Ⓑ Ⓒ Ⓓ	17 Ⓐ Ⓑ Ⓒ Ⓓ	32 Ⓐ Ⓑ Ⓒ Ⓓ	47 Ⓐ Ⓑ Ⓒ Ⓓ
3 Ⓐ Ⓑ Ⓒ Ⓓ	18 Ⓐ Ⓑ Ⓒ Ⓓ	33 Ⓐ Ⓑ Ⓒ Ⓓ	48 Ⓐ Ⓑ Ⓒ Ⓓ
4 Ⓐ Ⓑ Ⓒ Ⓓ	19 Ⓐ Ⓑ Ⓒ Ⓓ	34 Ⓐ Ⓑ Ⓒ Ⓓ	49 Ⓐ Ⓑ Ⓒ Ⓓ
5 Ⓐ Ⓑ Ⓒ Ⓓ	20 Ⓐ Ⓑ Ⓒ Ⓓ	35 Ⓐ Ⓑ Ⓒ Ⓓ	50 Ⓐ Ⓑ Ⓒ Ⓓ
6 Ⓐ Ⓑ Ⓒ Ⓓ	21 Ⓐ Ⓑ Ⓒ Ⓓ	36 Ⓐ Ⓑ Ⓒ Ⓓ	51 Ⓐ Ⓑ Ⓒ Ⓓ
7 Ⓐ Ⓑ Ⓒ Ⓓ	22 Ⓐ Ⓑ Ⓒ Ⓓ	37 Ⓐ Ⓑ Ⓒ Ⓓ	52 Ⓐ Ⓑ Ⓒ Ⓓ
8 Ⓐ Ⓑ Ⓒ Ⓓ	23 Ⓐ Ⓑ Ⓒ Ⓓ	38 Ⓐ Ⓑ Ⓒ Ⓓ	53 Ⓐ Ⓑ Ⓒ Ⓓ
9 Ⓐ Ⓑ Ⓒ Ⓓ	24 Ⓐ Ⓑ Ⓒ Ⓓ	39 Ⓐ Ⓑ Ⓒ Ⓓ	54 Ⓐ Ⓑ Ⓒ Ⓓ
10 Ⓐ Ⓑ Ⓒ Ⓓ	25 Ⓐ Ⓑ Ⓒ Ⓓ	40 Ⓐ Ⓑ Ⓒ Ⓓ	55 Ⓐ Ⓑ Ⓒ Ⓓ
11 Ⓐ Ⓑ Ⓒ Ⓓ	26 Ⓐ Ⓑ Ⓒ Ⓓ	41 Ⓐ Ⓑ Ⓒ Ⓓ	56 Ⓐ Ⓑ Ⓒ Ⓓ
12 Ⓐ Ⓑ Ⓒ Ⓓ	27 Ⓐ Ⓑ Ⓒ Ⓓ	42 Ⓐ Ⓑ Ⓒ Ⓓ	57 Ⓐ Ⓑ Ⓒ Ⓓ
13 Ⓐ Ⓑ Ⓒ Ⓓ	28 Ⓐ Ⓑ Ⓒ Ⓓ	43 Ⓐ Ⓑ Ⓒ Ⓓ	58 Ⓐ Ⓑ Ⓒ Ⓓ
14 Ⓐ Ⓑ Ⓒ Ⓓ	29 Ⓐ Ⓑ Ⓒ Ⓓ	44 Ⓐ Ⓑ Ⓒ Ⓓ	59 Ⓐ Ⓑ Ⓒ Ⓓ
15 Ⓐ Ⓑ Ⓒ Ⓓ	30 Ⓐ Ⓑ Ⓒ Ⓓ	45 Ⓐ Ⓑ Ⓒ Ⓓ	60 Ⓐ Ⓑ Ⓒ Ⓓ

SAMPLE

EDI | International House | Siskin Parkway East | Middlemarch Business Park | Coventry | CV3 4PE | UK
Tel. +44 (0) 8707 202909 | Fax +44 (0) 2476 516566 | Email. enquiries@ediplc.com | www.ediplc.com

Company Registration No. 3914767.   Registered Office: International House   Siskin Parkway East   Middlemarch Business Park   Coventry   CV3 4PE

ASNX0998R

LISTENING TEST 1

Listening Test 1 Part 1

Instructions to the candidate

Part 1 consists of ten multiple choice questions, 1-10. Listen to the questions and mark the correct answer, A, B or C, on your answer sheet. The questions are NOT printed.

Example

 1.01 Listen to the example question. Which is the correct answer?

As you heard, the question is 'Have you talked to Mr Izzard yet?' This sort of question requires a *yes/no* response, so the answer must be C, 'No, he went on holiday yesterday.'

Have you talked to Mr Izzard yet?

    A: Well, I don't know him.

    B: He's our local sales representative.

    C: No, he went on holiday yesterday.

Now listen to the CD for Listening Test 1 Part 1 and answer the questions.

Listening Test 1 Part 2

Instructions to the candidate

Part 2 consists of 20 multiple choice questions, 11-30. Read the question and the four possible answers, then listen to the conversation and choose the correct answer, A, B, C or D.

For example, read the question below and the four possible answers.

Example

How much does one shirt cost?

    A £10.00
    B £15.00
    C £12.50
    D £20.50

 1.12 Now listen to the conversation and choose the correct answer.

The correct answer is B; one shirt costs £15, so you would fill in 'B' on the answer sheet. You have ten seconds to read each question, and then you will hear the conversation or announcement. Look at the answer sheet and find where you should start filling in the answers for Part 2.

Now listen to the CD for Listening Test 1 Part 2 and answer the questions.

Questions and answers

11 How many jobs could be lost?
    A 10,000
    B 3
    C 3 million
    D none

12 What problem did the company have?
    A The company only made a profit of £8 million.
    B The company sells more than 100 products.
    C The two brothers have problems.
    D The company's bank has caused difficulties.

13 When does this offer start?
    A in the autumn
    B £1,000
    C next year
    D June

14 Why is there a budget of £100?
  A The relatives have not given you enough
     money.
  B There is not much money available.
  C There is no money for a holiday.
  D The house is not clean enough.

15 Why is the person concerned?
  A The person has not had a holiday for
     3 months.
  B The person's phone is not working.
  C The person has not received a recorded
     message.
  D The person can't get any help.

16 What can you buy cheaply online?
  A up to 15%
  B toys
  C good things
  D free delivery

17 Why does the second speaker have money
   with him?
  A Some cash is helpful.
  B He is travelling.
  C He has just come back from the United
     States.
  D He needs to get a taxi.

18 What is the effect of the pound's value?
  A The banks will worry.
  B The economy will improve.
  C Interest rates will be cut.
  D The dollar will become more important.

19 What do many companies in the UK do?
  A Give workers public holidays.
  B Give workers 2 weeks' holiday each
     year.
  C Give workers payment on public
     holidays.
  D Give workers a holiday when they start
     work.

20 What does the speaker think should
   happen?
  A She should be more careful.
  B The bank should be more helpful.
  C She should get her money back.
  D She should wait a month.

21 What is the man concerned about?
  A The bank has lost interest.
  B He might lose his account.
  C He can't write a cheque.
  D His bank has not replied to him.

22 When was the most difficult period in the
   man's business life?
  A When the company was set up.
  B When he worked for Tony Smith.
  C since 1994
  D since he met Tony Smith

23 What had a negative effect on the company
   last year?
  A There were too many passengers.
  B The new planes were too expensive.
  C The price of fuel has gone up.
  D Profits are bad.

24 What area of the financial market is the
   speaker talking about?
  A property costs
  B decreasing interest rates
  C saving money with the bank
  D interest in money

25 What is unusual about JSN?
  A The owners work in the stores.
  B Top managers do not know the owners.
  C The company is 40 years old.
  D The company is run by 2 brothers.

26 What is a disadvantage of this holiday if
   you wish to travel alone?
  A The hotel is more expensive.
  B The tours are guided.
  C You can choose the airport.
  D Dinner is not included.

27 How often does the company director travel
   abroad?
  A frequently
  B every day
  C never
  D unknown

28 Where are most of the company's full-time
   workers employed?
  A worldwide
  B in different businesses
  C in a world-famous building
  D in London

29 Why is Baasom so successful?
  A It has stores in London and Los Angeles.
  B It is popular all over the world.
  C It makes a lot of money.
  D It sells only luxury products.

30 How long must you register for, to receive
   the paper?
  A until you spend £100
  B for at least 6 months
  C when you phone the company
  D 2 weeks

LISTENING TEST 1

Further practice and guidance

Part 1 Listening

You will need to refer to the recording scripts on page 115 in order to complete these exercises.

Part 1 of the test focuses on your ability to understand questions and answers. It is very important that you listen for 'clues' to help you hear the question correctly. Verb forms and the correct question word will help you.

Always listen carefully for the verb form. Listen out for past or future time markers, or if it refers to something still going on. For example, 'I walk to work' shows present time and something you probably do every day, while 'I walked to work' is in the past. 'I'm walking to work' could be something you are doing as you are speaking, or even something you are planning to do very soon.

Exercise 1

Look at question 1 and note the verb forms. What time do they probably refer to?

_____

Exercise 2

Let's revise some tenses. Fill in the gaps with either the correct form of the verb in brackets, or the name of the tense. Refer to previous Further practice and guidance sections for help if necessary.

Example sentence	Tense
He _____ (work) from 9-5.	Present simple
I'm replying to the letter at the moment.	Present _____
Yesterday I stayed late at the office.	_____
The boss _____ (speak) when he was interrupted.	Past continuous
The office has never been so busy.	_____
Sales _____ (increase) this year.	Present perfect continuous
I _____ (complete) this report soon.	'Going to' future
I _____ (fly) to our Rome office at the weekend.	Present continuous future
My supervisor _____ (give) me some more work.	'Will' future

Exercise 3

Which questions have verb forms which refer to something still going on at the time of speaking?

_____

Exercise 4

Which questions have verb forms which refer to something which is always true or an event which happens regularly?

_____

Listen carefully and make sure you know the difference in sound AND meaning between:

Where	How	Why	Who	What	When

Exercise 5

Students often understand generally what they hear, but mishear the wrong question-word, and so give the wrong answer to the wrong question. What information do the following question words need? Match the questions with the kind of answer needed.

a time	a place	an explanation	a person

a) Where is it?   _____

b) When is it?   _____

c) Who is it?   _____

d) How do you do it?   _____

Exercise 6

Look at these questions and responses. Can you match them?

a) Where is the departmental meeting?   1) It's in the main conference room.

b) When is the meeting?   2) Mr Jones

c) Who is the new Chairman?   3) Look at the instruction book.

d) How do I install this new program?   4) It's on Thursday.

e) Who do I get the new sales figures from?   5) Ms Smith has a copy.

f) How do I access this file?   6) You need a password.

Exercise 7

Put the questions into groups depending on the question word you hear, and think about the kind of answer needed.

Who questions: _____

What questions: _____

When questions: _____

Where questions: _____

How questions: _____

Notice that we can also have questions which require 'Yes' or 'No' as an answer. There are no question words in the question and the verb comes before the subject. Look at these examples, and see how you can answer the questions with either 'Yes' or 'No'.

Do you know the new password?	Yes, it's 1062.
Did you work late last night?	No, I didn't.

Notice that we sometimes give extra information, or confirm or deny the statement with a verb form similar to a tag phrase.

Exercise 8

Answer these questions in the same way as the examples above.

a) Have you read the report? (yes)   _____

b) Did you attend the conference yesterday? (no)   _____

c) Do you know the end-of-year results? (no)   _____

d) Were you tired after the meeting? (yes)   _____

e) Have you finished yet? (no)

Part 2 Listening

Part 2 of the test looks more traditional as you are given the question and then have to decide on the correct answer from four options. If you read the questions carefully, it may be possible to see that one of the answers is probably not very likely before you even hear the information.

Exercise 1

Look at the second question in Part 2, question 12. The question asks about problems in a company, so the answer will probably be a negative one. What kind of problems might a company have?

_____

Exercise 2

In the same question, is there a 'positive' answer?

_____

Exercise 3

In the same question, is there an answer which might seem less relevant to the question?

_____

Immediately you can see that two answers seem less possible, but that does not mean that you do not need to listen for all the information – it means you can listen more carefully with some knowledge in your head, and listen out for what the speaker might say about '100 products' or about 'two brothers'.

Exercise 4

With this information and still without looking at the recording script, can you 'guess' a possible answer before you hear the audio?

_____

Exercise 5

Look at question 11. Are there any answers there which are 'less likely'? Do the same for questions 16 and 27.

Question 11 _____

Question 16 _____

Question 27 _____

A lot of these questions revolve around numbers, so let's look at writing numbers in figures and words in more detail.

Exercise 6

Write these numbers in words.

a) 50   _____

b) 15   _____

c) 15,000 _____

d) 11,555 _____

e) 535   _____

Exercise 7

Can you write these words as numbers?

a) Three hundred and fifty five thousand _____

b) Four hundred and fifty _____

c) Sixty two thousand _____

d) Twenty five million _____

e) Thirty eight thousand and three _____

Exercise 8

How many ways are there to say '0'?

_____

Don't be distracted by the content of what you hear. Remember this is an English test and you do not have to have expert knowledge of the money markets, for example, to be able to answer the questions set.

Exercise 9

Let's look at some money vocabulary. Can you work out what these words are? The vowel letters (aeiou) are missing.

a) w-ll-t   _____   b) -ns-r-nc-   _____

c) -c-n-my   _____   d) -nt-r-st r-t-s _____

e) b-nk ch-rg-s   _____   f) -cc- -nt   _____

g) st-ck -xch-ng- _____   h) -nv-stm-nt   _____

i) c-sh   _____   j) ch-q- -   _____

k) c-rr-ncy   _____

LISTENING TEST 2

Listening Test 2 Part 1

Instructions to the candidate

Part 1 consists of ten multiple choice questions, 1-10. Listen to the questions and mark the correct answer, A, B or C, on your answer sheet. The questions are NOT printed.

Example

 1.33 Listen to the example question. Which is the correct answer?

As you heard, the question is 'What are you doing?' As the question word is 'what', the answer is probably a noun, so the answer must be A, 'The accounts'.

What are you doing?

A: the accounts

B: on the left

C: not yet

Now listen to the CD for Listening Test 2 Part 1 and answer the questions.

Listening Test 2 Part 2

Instructions to the candidate

Part 2 consists of 20 multiple choice questions, 11-30. Read the question and the four possible answers, then listen to the conversation and choose the correct answer, A, B, C or D.

For example, read the question below and the four possible answers.

Example

How much does one shirt cost?
- **A** £10.00
- **B** £15.00
- **C** £12.50
- **D** £20.50

 1.44 Now listen to the conversation and choose the correct answer.

The correct answer is B; one shirt costs £15, so you would fill in 'B' on the answer sheet. You have ten seconds to read each question, and then you will hear the conversation or announcement. Look at the answer sheet and find where you should start filling in the answers for Part 2.

Now listen to the CD for Listening Test 2 Part 2 and answer the questions.

Questions and answers

11 What does the Bank do?
- **A** sponsor sport
- **B** entertain the public
- **C** criticize the government
- **D** help celebrities

12 What does the second speaker do?
- **A** work in a factory
- **B** work for Berriedale
- **C** work in the music industry
- **D** work in Wales

13 Why is the oil company for sale?
- **A** There is a problem with its partners.
- **B** There are worldwide financial problems.
- **C** There are investment difficulties for the company.
- **D** There is no money left in the company.

14 What does the first speaker want to do?

    A spend money
    B save money
    C earn money
    D pay money

15 What is the advantage of this bag?

    A It has a lock on its computer pocket.
    B It can be taken on planes.
    C It organizes your work.
    D It's the right price.

16 Why did the second speaker visit the supermarket?

    A He read an article about it.
    B He wanted to save money.
    C It's near his house.
    D It produces its own bread.

17 What is a negative effect of losing your job?

    A You can feel depressed.
    B You have no time to spend with your family.
    C You lose your identity.
    D You can't catch up with colleagues.

18 What is the biggest difference between the UK and the US magazine markets?

    A A men's magazine is very unpopular.
    B Home improvements are not very interesting.
    C Fewer magazines are being read in the US.
    D There are 82 magazines on the market.

19 What are the speakers planning to do?

    A stay in a hotel
    B go to the theatre
    C have a meal
    D visit France

20 What will happen to the celebrity's company in the future?

    A It will make £4 million.
    B It will become a television company.
    C It will remain his company.
    D It will work with 2 other companies.

21 What did the first speaker do?

    A She took a holiday.
    B She spent too much money.
    C She took a new job.
    D She made a complaint.

22 What are the viewers being encouraged to do?

    A save money
    B watch more TV
    C telephone Channel 10
    D use more energy

23 What does the second speaker consider unfair?

    A They have only 25% of sales.
    B Other supermarkets were looked at.
    C The same things have not been compared.
    D Other supermarkets sell different sizes.

24 What does the second colleague recommend?

    A putting money into his account
    B being satisfied in 6 months
    C moving a bank account
    D doubling his money

25 What is the second speaker talking about?

    A her job
    B what time she finishes work
    C her favourite sport
    D how she avoids stress

26 Why didn't the woman get the job?

    A She didn't prepare for the interview.
    B The company wanted to employ somebody new.
    C She decided she didn't want the promotion.
    D The company had already decided on somebody else.

27 What is a benefit of Deep South's plans?

    A The friends can find a branch more easily.
    B There will be more employment.
    C The food will improve.
    D The company will be more popular.

28 Who might be suitable for the award of Secretary of the Year?

    A a third colleague
    B the second speaker's secretary
    C the first speaker
    D somebody who is motivated

29 What is the man looking for?

    A a loan
    B a job
    C the sales advisor
    D the Rockton Bank

30 What are the friends going to do?

    A try and get help to find a job
    B register at college
    C write their CVs
    D visit some large companies

LISTENING TEST 2

Further practice and guidance

Part 1 Listening

You will need to refer to the recording scripts on page 115 in order to complete these exercises.

Be careful with numbers which are given. Listen carefully for any double numbers such as 22 or 44 and so on. Pay particular attention to numbers which can sound similar, for example 13 and 30, 14 and 40. Especially on the phone, people often say, for example, 'fifteen' = 'one five' to be clear.

Exercise 1

What are different ways of saying these times in words?

a) 0530 _____

b) 0545 _____

c) 0830 _____

d) 1115 _____

Exercise 2

Look at these words. Some of them are spelt incorrectly. Can you spell them all correctly? Clue: four of them are spelt incorrectly.

a) accomodation   _____

b) adress   _____

c) independent   _____

d) recieved   _____

e) seperate   _____

f) recommend   _____

g) altogether   _____

h) permanent   _____

Exercise 3

Make sure you know what CAPITAL letters and initials are. My initials in CAPITAL letters are VLL. What are yours?

_____

Part 2 Listening

Exercise 1

The questions often contain clues about the subject matter of the listening. Refer to the questions below. What is the listening probably about?

Question 13 _____

Question 15 _____

Question 19 _____

Question 20 _____

Exercise 2

Scanning is the technique for finding specific information. Look at the questions in Part 2 of the test, and find the following words and phrases. All the answers are in the A/B/C/D parts. Write the question numbers.

a) worldwide financial problems   _____

b) 25%   _____

c) bread   _____

d) Channel 10   _____

e) home improvements   _____

f) 2 other companies   _____

g) made a complaint   _____

h) depressed   _____

i) find a job   _____

j) promotion   _____

Exercise 3

Which questions seem to be about the following subjects? This is an opportunity for skimming: understanding the gist.

a) work   _____

b) a product   _____

c) the media   _____

d) money   _____

e) people and activities   _____

Exercise 4

Read the definitions below. All the words appear in the listening test. What are they?

a) A word which means 'say negative things about someone'.   _____

b) A word which means 'a famous person'.   _____

c) A word which means 'someone you work with'.   _____

d) A word which means 'a part of a company or a part of a tree'.   _____

e) A word which means 'get ready for'.   _____

f) A word which means 'suggest doing something'.   _____

g) A word which means 'advantage'.   _____

Skills: | *avoiding distractors* |

Let's look at how you can work out which information will distract you from choosing the correct answer. Look at the first question in Part 2 of the test.

You can see that there is a different verb in each of the possible answers (sponsors/ entertains/ criticizes/ helps). When you listen to the information, you should listen for these words AND which noun they are connected to (sport/ the public/ government/ celebrities). Then you can choose the correct combination, which will give you the correct answer.

Here are some examples of other things which may lead you to give the wrong answer.

Exercise 5

a) What is the same in the possible answers in question 12?

_____

b) What is the same in question 14?

_____

c) What do you notice about the possible answers in question 16?

_____

d) Looking at question 15, which answer seems unlikely? Why?

_____

e) Looking at question 22, which answer seems unlikely? Why?

_____

Vocabulary: | *advice* |

Exercise 6

Let's have a look at the language of advice. Which questions do these phrases come from? Refer to the recording scripts.

a) What can I do?   _____

b) Do you have any ideas?   _____

c) Why don't you …   _____

d) What can we …?   _____

Exercise 7

Look at the following definitions. Match them with the verbs of advice in the box.

urge   advise   suggest   persuade   encourage

a) put forward an idea   _____

b) recommend strongly that someone does something   _____

c) get someone to do something   _____

d) give someone advice   _____

e) give support or hope to someone   _____

Exercise 8

Use the verbs of advice to complete the following sentences. Change the form if necessary.

a) The employee _____ a plan to improve sales.

b) The head of department _____ the team to work harder.

c) We were all _____ to do some overtime because of the amount of work.

d) We want to _____ as many customers as possible to buy our new product.

e) The IT manager _____ us to upgrade our computer system to make our work easier.

SPEAKING TEST 1

Optional

Instructions to the candidate

- You have up to five minutes to prepare for your examination by looking at the pictures and reading the questions.

- Do not write anything during the preparation time.

- At the start of the examination the examiner will ask you some questions about yourself (two minutes).

- You will then have five minutes to talk about the topic, using the pictures to help you. The examiner will ask you questions to help you.

- Give this sheet back to the examiner at the end of the examination.

The Topic: COMMUTING

- Describe the picture.

- How do commuters travel to work every day in your country?

- Why do people travel to work like this?

- How much and how soon do you think 'new technology' will mean that people will no longer have to travel to the office every day?

- What are the advantages/disadvantages of working in a big city?

- What effect does travelling like this every day have on people and the environment?

- Where would you prefer to work? Why?

SPEAKING TEST 1

Further practice and guidance

Exercise 1

Can you answer the following questions about the test itself? Clue: all the answers are in the 'Instructions to the Candidate' section.

a) How long do you have to prepare for the test? _____

b) How many parts are there in the test? _____

c) Do you have to write anything during the test? _____

d) Who chooses the subject you will talk about? _____

Exercise 2

Think carefully about the kinds of things you might want to know if you met someone for the first time. These are the things the examiner might ask you in the first two minutes of the test. Write down four questions.

_____

_____

_____

_____

Exercise 3

Do you know the kind of things you might say in reply? Write the responses to your questions in exercise 2.

_____

_____

_____

_____

_____

If you can, practise these questions and possible answers with another class member or a friend.

Exercise 4

What are your plans for the future? How will you try and achieve those aims?

This question is a chance for you to think about what you want to do in the future, and how you can achieve it: what qualifications you need, how to get those qualifications, what experience you have, what kind of person you are and so on. Write your ideas below.

_____

_____

_____

_____

Exercise 5

What sort of work experience have you had – e.g. helping a relative in a shop; working during the holidays? Write a few sentences below describing what you did.

_____

_____

Exercise 6

Think of three disadvantages of commuting.

_____

_____

Exercise 7

What are the big cities or commercial areas in your country? Write down a few descriptive words or phrases. Compare them to any areas of countryside which you have visited.

City	Countryside

Exercise 8

Think of five words to describe the people on a commuter train.

_____   _____   _____   _____   _____

Exercise 9

How do commuters travel to work every day in your country? What are the possible ways? Here is one – by bus – can you think of any more? The first letter of each answer is given.

a) by t __ __ __ __   b) by t __ __ __   c) by c __ __   d) by b __ __ __

e) by s __ __ __ __ __ (this is an American word for b)   f) on f __ __ __

Notice the last one: it is ON and not BY.

Exercise 10

Why do people travel to work like this? There could be a lot of reasons, which might depend on where the worker lives. Can you think of some of them?

_____

_____

_____

_____

SPEAKING TEST 2

Optional

Instructions to the candidate

- You have up to five minutes to prepare for your examination by looking at the pictures and reading the questions.

- Do not write anything during the preparation time.

- At the start of the examination the examiner will ask you some questions about yourself (two minutes).

- You will then have five minutes to talk about the topic, using the pictures to help you. The examiner will ask you questions to help you.

- Give this sheet back to the examiner at the end of the examination.

The Topic: TECHNOLOGY

- Describe the pictures and any differences you can see.

- How do offices look in your country? What kind of buildings can you see in the commercial and banking centres?

- In the future, do you think it will be necessary to travel to offices in order to work?

- What disadvantages might there be for business in using new technology?

- Do you think modern society is wise to rely so much on technology? Why/Why not?

SPEAKING TEST 2

Further practice and guidance

Remember that the first questions in the warm-up are to relax you, and for the examiner to get to know you a little. The assessor is sympathetic to you and wants to see what you can do, NOT to find out what you don't know. Don't forget this is a language test, not a test of knowledge.

Exercise 1

Can you remember how long the warm-up is? _____

Think of your own study or work experience. Do you know the English names of everything you work with? For example, do you know the names of everything on your desk?

Exercise 2

Look at this picture of a desk. Write the names of the labelled items.

a) _____ b) _____ c) _____

d) _____ e) _____ f) _____

Can you think of any other things you use every day when you are at work or studying? Why not look around each day and make a list in your head, or write down things you see. This will help you to revise vocabulary and keep it fresh in your mind.

Exercise 3

Write down three things you might see in the following situations.

a) in the street _____ _____ _____

b) in the office _____ _____ _____

c) in a café _____ _____ _____

Exercise 4

What do you do in a typical day? Complete the sentences below.

In the morning I usually _____

In the afternoon I sometimes _____

In the evening I _____

Exercise 5

Do you use any technology to relax, for example mp3 player/mobile phone/computer games? Can you think of some of the negative as well as the positive things about these items of technology? Complete the table below.

Positive	Negative

Exercise 6

How can you join the ideas above while you are speaking? Complete the sentences with the words below – they are called linking words. Pay attention to punctuation.

> however   also   but   and   because

a) I enjoy playing computer games _____ surfing the internet.

b) I take my mp3 player everywhere _____ I love listening to music.

c) Technology nowadays is very efficient and useful in all our lives. _____ , it can be quite expensive.

d) I download a lot of music from the internet, but I _____ buy CDs.

e) I love my laptop _____ I hate it when it crashes!

Exercise 7

Using the sentences above, complete the rules about linking words.

a) We use _____ to join two similar ideas together.

b) We use _____ to contrast two ideas.

c) We use _____ to contrast two ideas. It must start a sentence or be used with a comma before and after.

d) We use _____ to give a reason for something.

e) We use _____ to add another piece of information.

Exercise 8

Using your ideas from exercise 5, write three sentences using linking words.

_____

_____

_____

Try to talk with another class member about this topic, and perhaps make a few notes about what you talked about – or even record the conversation so that you can listen to it again. If you don't have a classmate to speak to, recording yourself answering the questions and listening back is a really good way of improving your speaking skills. What words did you get wrong? Should you have spoken more quickly? Did you make any mistakes? Now repeat the exercise and listen again. Did you do better this time?

ANSWER KEY

Common skills

Exercise 1

1B 2B 3B 4A 5B

Exercise 2

a) 16-65

b) Motivated and reliable

c) £6.50

d) Email them (derhamcouriers@pavilion.com)

e) 2108

Exercise 3

Model answer

Information

1 Day + time

2 Place

3 Subject

4 Speaker

5 Breaks

Exercise 4

Model answer

Details

1 Tuesday 21 August 1430-1800

2 Works Café

3 Working with Customers

4 Mr Jones (HR)

5 Tea and Coffee at 4pm

Exercise 5

Model Answer

Please phone Mr Jones urgently Tuesday re: recent order.

Exercise 6

a) Consensus = agreement

b) Exaggerate = say that something is larger or more successful than it really is

c) Gauge = an instrument that measures the level of something

d) Omit = leave something out

e) Yield = profit or financial gain

Exercise 7

a) loaves

b) deer

c) chose

d) put (me) in (touch) with

e) put up

Exercise 8

a) 2

b) 1

c) 1

d) 2

e) 1

f) 1

g) 2

Exercise 9

a) *The carpenter accidentally nailed the nail through his nail.*

The carpenter accidentally hit the metal spike through the hard part at the end of his finger.

b) *He parked next to the park.*

He placed his car next to the green area.

c) *I saw him saw the wood with his saw.*

I watched him cut the wood with a tool used for dividing wood into pieces.

d) *The girl with the wavy hair waved as she disappeared under the waves.*

The girl, whose hair was not straight, put her hand in the air and moved it, as she disappeared under the moving water.

e) *The little boy was trying to tie his tie.*

The little boy tried to put together the long piece of cloth often worn with a shirt by males.

Exercise 10

a) ~~assent~~ ascent

b) ~~pair~~ pear

c) ~~souls~~ soles

d) ~~boy~~ buoy

e) ~~flower~~ flour

f) ~~hair~~ hare

g) ~~duel~~ dual

h) ~~rain~~ reign

Exercise 11

You are given headings to fill in which don't appear in a letter, so you wouldn't begin 'Dear ..' and end 'Yours …', as in a letter. A memo is also shorter and has a subject header, requiring you to state exactly what the memo is about.

Exercise 12

You are the Manager and you are writing to your Deputy Manager.

Exercise 13

You will be polite and friendly because you work with him and want him to do something, but you will also be certain of what you want him to do and expect a positive response.

The phrases in the task showing your attitude and style are:

Manager   Deputy Manager
Check how far advanced …

ask him for …   Make sure he knows …   You want information from him as soon as possible

You consider this matter very important …

Exercise 14

The memo is asking about the arrangements for an Open Day at your company.

The key points are:

Timetable?

Where?

Who?

Breaks?

The following also need to be included:

Your availability

A reply ASAP

The importance of the matter

Exercise 15

The phrases taken from the text can be rewritten as follows, although you may have other, equally correct answers.

a) … how much work has already been done/how many arrangements have already been made …

b) the day's programme/the programme for the day

c) where the visitors will be shown

d) refreshment breaks/ the plans for breaks

e) I will take part/I'm in the office/ I'm free …

f) this is an important day for the company…

Exercise 16

Model Answer

MEMORANDUM

TO: John Irvine (Deputy Manager)

FROM: Julian Williams (Manager)

DATE: 21 10 09

SUBJECT: Open Day visit

Please let me know as soon as possible what arrangements have already been made for the upcoming visit to our company. As you know this is an important day for the company and for our future business, so it is essential that everything goes as smoothly as possible.

Please send me ASAP a draft programme for the day. Please include information about where the visitors will be shown, so that those Departments can be thoroughly prepared. It is also important to know who the visitors will be meeting, so that our staff can be fully briefed.

In addition, please include details of refreshment breaks, so that the catering staff can be ready with tea and coffee as required.

Finally, please note that I am in the office on the day of the visit, and am therefore free to meet our visitors at any time during the day.

I wait to hear from you.

(153 words)

Exercise 17

a) The name of a market is required.

b) A number is required.

c) The name of the market is required.

Exercise 18

a) The titles across the page are: Change On Week, Current Level, 12-mth High and 12-mth Low.

b) They are all names of World Share Markets.

Exercise 19

a) There are 14 figures with minus (-) signs, all in the Change On Week column.

b) There are five names which also have numbers in them: (FTSE 100; S&P 500; Tokyo Nikkei 225; Paris Cac 40 and FTSE Eurofirst 300).

c) The cities mentioned are Tokyo; Frankfurt; Paris; Bombay and Shanghai.

Exercise 20

1 Hang Seng

2 FTSE A/S Yield %

3 Hang Seng

4 FTSE A/S Yield %

5 FTSE A/S Yield %

6 Dow Jones Industrial and Tokyo Nikkei 225

7 Hang Seng

8 Paris Cac 40 and Australia All Ords

9 143

10 11015

11 Dow Jones World

12 -185

13 Industrial/World

14 4

15 5

16 1

17 Weekly

18 FTSE A/S Yield %

19 S&P 500

20 Shanghai Composite

Exercise 21

The question word is 'Where' so a place is required for the answer.

Exercise 22

The correct answer is 1C.

Exercise 23

a) What are you doing at the moment?

b) When do you finish your course? / When are you finishing your course?

Exercise 24

The correct answer is A.

Question 1: Where does it/ the last bus to the station leave/go from?

Question 2: How much does it cost?

Exercise 25

The correct answer is B.

Question 1: How much does it cost?

Question 2: Do you have / Can I see / Can I have your ticket?

Exercise 26

The question word is 'What' so a fact or name of something is required.

The correct answer is A.

Exercise 27

Distracting information is 'good bargains' and the information about sofas.

Exercise 28

The correct answer is D. Distracting information is 'increased passenger numbers', 'planes delivered last year', and 'cost of fuel decreased'. The information you need is right at the end of the listening.

READING AND WRITING TEST 1

QUESTION 1

MODEL ANSWER

> ODDS Tools Manchester Street London N2 03B
>
> 5th March 2009
>
> Mr Smith
> DBC Manufacturing
> Sterling Road
> Leeds LE7 9BS
>
> Dear Mr Smith,
>
> We are very pleased to confirm receipt of your recent order for 300 examples of Machine Tool No. 5014, which arrived on 03/03/09.
>
> Unfortunately, I have to inform you that this particular model has been in short supply recently, due to some minor production problems in our supplier's factory, which, as you know, is situated in Finland. The company has now resolved this problem.

> We are able to offer 150 examples of the model for immediate despatch, with the remainder guaranteed to follow in 3 weeks.
>
> We apologize for any inconvenience this may cause, and hope that this will be acceptable to you. As a goodwill gesture, we would be happy to offer you a discount of 15% on your next order.
>
> We very much hope that this will be satisfactory for you, and look forward to working with you again in future.
>
> Please do not hesitate to contact me if you wish to discuss this matter further.
>
> Yours sincerely,
>
> ODDS Tools

(167 words)

QUESTION 2

Quotes are suggested answers only, and other wording might be acceptable.

1 TRUE	company's famous products/ fortieth anniversary
2 TRUE	(control) within Menn family/ William consultant
3 FALSE	diversified/ French operation controlled from UK
4 TRUE	skilled and unskilled (workers)/ France, Hong Kong
5 FALSE	'modern' feel / control within Menn family
6 FALSE	economic situation / job cuts avoided
7 TRUE	equipment design/(recently won) award for original design
8 FALSE	almost instant success/ thousand workers
9 FALSE	William now retired/ consultant sometimes
10 FALSE	special events/ performance in markets

QUESTION 3

1 Venture (£3,815)	11 petrol + diesel
2 Tourer	12 central locking
3 all/4	13 LPG (liquid petroleum gas)
4 alloy wheels	14 1 (Venture)
5 Tourer	15 Veron/£1,545
6 Tiger (2 extras)	16 No (all cars have CD players)
7 3 (Veron/Venture/ Tourer)	17 Tiger
8 £7,795 (Tiger)	18 0 / none
9 Veron + Venture	19 16"
10 Tourer	20 Tiger (4 features)

QUESTION 4

Name of delegate	Flight	Arrival time in London	Hotel	Contact details
1 KICKI BACKMAN	SAS 707	1830	GRAND HOTEL	07743 112233, AFTER 2000
2 ANNE SMITH	TO MANCHESTER / UNKNOWN	2330	GREAT WESTERN HOTEL	HER COLLEAGUE, ROOM 333
3 JULIAN WOOD	NO FLIGHT	1500	OAK TREE HOTEL	EMAIL/HIS SECRETARY
4 JOHN COX	787	2000	GRAND HOTEL	EMAIL TODAY, THEN HOTEL

READING AND WRITING TEST 1
Further practice and guidance

Exercise 1
a) 2

b) 1

c) 3

Exercise 2
Suggested answers

a) Thank you for your recent order, dated ….

b) Transport problems; strike action; staff illness etc.

c) In one week's time, for example.

d) A ten per cent discount on their next order, for example.

Exercise 3
receipt

Exercise 4
a) foreign

b) weird

c) ceiling

Exercise 5
a) ✓

b) approximately

c) separate

d) ✓

e) recommend

Exercise 6
a) Unfortunately, I have to inform you …

b) We hope this is suitable.

c) for immediate despatch

d) As a gesture of goodwill …

e) …if you wish to discuss this matter further.

Exercise 7
The language is quite formal with long phrases and unusual words such as 'gesture'.

Exercise 8
You should have highlighted or underlined these names in the text every time they appeared:

Irvine and William Menn

UK, France, Hong Kong, Europe

Exercise 9
You should have highlighted or underlined these numbers and dates in the text every time they appeared:

1971; 1990; 1984; fortieth

Exercise 10
a) William was known as 'the design genius'.

b) It was successful 'due to its imaginative ideas and state-of-the-art equipment design'.

c) William is now retired but 'acts as a much-valued consultant from time to time'.

d) The company's name was changed to Mennco in 1984.

e) Job cuts 'have been avoided so far'.

f) Next year is the company's fortieth anniversary and some special events are planned.

Exercise 11
Read the questions first, then refer to the information. It's a good idea to underline or highlight any key words that will help you answer the questions.

Exercise 12
You are normally being asked to pick out one fact.

Exercise 13
Complete the sentences so they are true for you.

a) I live in …

b) I'm an /a ….

c) I start work at …

d) I work for …

e) I work there because …

Exercise 14

a) The verb construction used for each question is 'do you'.

b) For 'he' and 'she', 'do you' becomes 'does he' and 'does she'.

Exercise 15

a) Where does she live?

b) What does she do?

c) When does she start work?

d) Who does she work for?

e) Why does she work there?

Exercise 16

a) Yes, I do. / No, I don't.

b) Yes, I am. / No, I'm not.

c) Yes, I do. / No, I don't.

d) Yes, I am. / No, I'm not.

Exercise 17

a) CD player and manual are the same.

b) Central locking, alloy wheels, liquid petroleum gas and flat-seat system are only mentioned once.

Exercise 18

a) Each of the adjectives has one syllable.

b) We add 'est' to make one-syllable adjectives into superlatives.

c) We add another 'n' or 'g' to an adjective that ends in 'n' or 'g' when it becomes superlative.

d) If an adjective already ends in 'e', we only add 'st' to make it superlative.

Exercise 19

a) There are two syllables in each adjective.

b) There are four syllables in the word 'intelligent': in-tell-i-gent.

c) We add 'most' before adjectives with three or more syllables.

d) We add 'iest' to adjectives that end in 'y', after removing the 'y'.

Exercise 20

a) He is the OLDEST boss I have worked for.

b) She is the MOST INTELLIGENT secretary in the company.

c) He is the BEST worker in the Department.

d) This is the SIMPLEST form to fill in.

Exercise 21

a) My office is the largest in the building.

b) This idea is the most practical solution.

c) This product is the most expensive.

d) The sales report is the worst this year.

Exercise 22

The three details that might require numbers are flight, arrival time and contact details.

Exercise 23

a) 707 is Kicki Backman's flight number.

b) This is Kicki Backman's contact telephone number.

c) 787 is John Cox's flight number.

d) This is the room number of Anne Smith's colleague, who is her contact.

Exercise 24

a) This is John Cox's arrival time in London, and the time after which Kicki Backman can be contacted. It is also the arrival time of Anne Smith's flight to Manchester.

b) This is the time Julian Wood arrives in London.

c) This is the time Anne Smith arrives in London.

Exercise 25

a) Kicki Backman and John Cox

b) –

c) Anne Smith

d) Julian Wood

Exercise 26

You should have highlighted:

Paragraph 1: Gothenburg and London

Paragraph 2: France, Manchester and London

Paragraph 3: Manchester

Paragraph 4: Stockholm

Exercise 27

will do/ will be doing

Exercise 28

At my office on Fridays, we **plan** our work for the following week. Next week I **am going to fly** to Rome for an important business conference, which the boss asked me to attend. I **am meeting** two important customers and I am sure it **will be** very interesting.

Exercise 29

a) contact

b) colleague

c) confirm

d) urgent

READING AND WRITING TEST 2

QUESTION 1

MODEL ANSWER

MEMORANDUM

TO: All colleagues – Complaints Dept

FROM: A Smith – HR

DATE: 21.08.09

SUBJECT: Training Day

Please note that the next training day for ALL members of the Complaints Department will take place on Saturday 26 September from 1000-1630.

As you are aware, the company prides itself on good customer relations. It aims to hold a training day every year, to keep staff updated with the latest skills. During the past year, however, the company has received some rather bad publicity in newspapers regarding the confused and slow handling of customer complaints.

As a result, we have no alternative but to make the training day COMPULSORY for all colleagues. Please contact your line manager if you have any problems with this.

The training will be held in the Conference Centre. On arrival, please report to Reception, where you will be given a badge and information telling you which group you have been allocated to.

The introductory talk will be in Macmillan Hall at 1030, followed by a coffee break at 1130. There will be a series of small group workshops until lunch, at 1300 in the main restaurant. The workshops will resume until the final session at 1600, in Macmillan Hall.

(184 words)

QUESTION 2

Quotes are suggested answers only, and other wording might be acceptable.

1 TRUE	enquiries doubled/ 21% increase in deposits
2 TRUE	reputation as 'safest bank'/ limited branches
3 FALSE	talk to real person / know customers
4 FALSE	£15,000 or less/ pay £40 (per month)
5 FALSE	£1.5 billion deposits/ £17.3 million in bonds
6 FALSE	managers know their customers/ remember details
7 FALSE	profts/ safe bonds and securities
8 TRUE	internet banking/ personal investment service
9 FALSE	profits until March 2009/ £17.3 million
10 TRUE	come and talk/ can do (for you)

QUESTION 3

1 HH and HH Extra
2 19"
3 £599.97
4 HH Extra
5 PWC and HH (15.6")
6 'Duo'
7 3 / three
8 2 GB
9 HH Extra
10 IMPR and the HH
11 1 / one
12 graphics card
13 limited stock
14 IMPR
15 phone
16 T3200
17 353
18 19"
19 nothing / free
20 discount

QUESTION 4

1
Name: ANN WARWICK
Age: 24
Length of experience: 2 YEARS
Contact details: 00127 721721
Languages: FRENCH

2
Name: BRIAN MACINTOSH
Age: 35
Length of experience: 7 YEARS
Contact details: britm@pavillon.com
Languages: CHINESE, FRENCH, GERMAN

3
Name: JONATHAN BAKER
Age: 27
Length of experience: 3 YEARS
Contact details: 020 333 1112
Languages spoken: PORTUGUESE

4
Name: HELEN RAWLINGS
Age: 21
Length of experience: 6 MONTHS
Contact details: 0210 345876
Languages spoken: AFRIKAANS, DUTCH

READING AND WRITING TEST 2
Further practice and guidance

Exercise 1

You should give all the necessary points clearly and concisely. For example, compare the long sentence and the shorter version below.

The training will take place between 10 a.m. and 4 p.m. on Saturday 26th July at Old Bank Hotel.

Training: 10-4pm Saturday 26th July at Old Bank Hotel

Exercise 2

The staff are giving up a day of their weekend for the training, so it is important that the memo sounds positive. For example, you could mention that this is an opportunity for staff to upgrade their skills, or keep up-to-date with customer service techniques. Stressing that the company values its staff, which is why it wants them trained, would also be a positive thing to say.

Exercise 3

Training Day

Exercise 4

a) colleagues
b) brief
c) compulsory
d) voluntary

Exercise 5

The training is probably needed if customers have complained, or if there has been some bad publicity about the company.

Exercise 6

a) You should have underlined the time, date and location of the training day.
b) In Model Answer A, you should have underlined nine short forms: *it's, It'll, it's, we're, 'Cos, can't, We'll, you'll* and *We'll*. There are no short forms in Model Answer B.
c) In Model Answer A, the three spelling mistakes are *costumers* (customers), *newpapers* (newspapers) and *usuaul* (usual).

Exercise 7

Model Answer A does not include the relevant information, and is not written in an appropriate style. Some of the language ('we're rubbish', 'some kind of lunch', 'there you are!') is unsuitable, as is the use of short forms. Spelling mistakes look unprofessional and should be avoided.

Model Answer B is the most suitable answer to the question. It uses the correct style with no spelling or grammar mistakes, and all the information is given clearly so we know the purpose, time, date and arrangements for the day.

Exercise 8

a) The bank is 'preparing to enter the market in a more conventional way'.
b) Its existing customers recommend new customers.
c) The bank's policy is one of 'cautious investment'.
d) There are a limited number of branches.

Exercise 9

The text sounds quite informative and friendly e.g. 'please come and talk', '[what we] can do for you'.

Exercise 10

a) sound
b) branch
c) ring

Exercise 11

suggested answers

£1.5 billion – the amount of customer deposits

£15,000 – the savings amount under which customers are charged for transactions

£17.3 million – pre-tax profits until March 2009

Exercise 12

a) reputation
b) reduce
c) customer
d) transaction
e) vast
f) tempt
g) state-of-the-art
h) conference

Exercise 13

Computers can be used for many things, but some examples include surfing the internet, playing music, watching films, sending emails and creating digital documents (Word files etc.).

Exercise 14

a) surf the internet
b) click the mouse
c) download music
d) scroll up or down
e) save a file
f) log in or out

Exercise 15

a) To check your email, you have to **log in**.
b) I save loads of money by **downloading music** from the internet.
c) Make sure you **save** your **file** before shutting down the computer.
d) I really should stop **surfing the internet** and start studying!

e) If you can't see the whole screen, you can **scroll up and down**.

f) **Click the mouse** on the file you want to open.

Exercise 16

You should have highlighted: *processor, GB memory, GB hard drive, widescreen, webcam, wireless connectivity* and *graphics card*.

Exercise 17

The box for HH Extra is longer than the others and contains more information.

Exercise 18

A lot of the information is repeated in each box e.g. amount of memory, processor, size of hard drive and screen.

Exercise 19

a) price of PWC

b) GB hard drive of IMPR

c) ref of IMPR

d) screen width of IMPR

e) GB memory of PWC

Exercise 20

a) Questions 2 and 3 ask for 'the largest screen' and 'the most expensive price'.

b) Questions 4, 9, 14 and 15 ask you to find something different about the computers.

c) Questions 2, 3, 7, 8, 11, 17 and 18 require a number in the answer.

Exercise 21

a) memory

b) phone

c) delivery

d) widescreen

e) limited

Exercise 22

You need to find five pieces of information about each person, and two of those require numbers – their age, and length of experience. Contact details might also require numbers.

Exercise 23

Suggested answers:

Name: What is your name?

Age: How old are you?

Length of experience: How much experience do you have?

Contact details: How can we contact you?

Languages: What foreign languages do you speak?

Exercise 24

Suggested answers:

a) What do you do in your free time? What are your interests and hobbies?

b) What are your ambitions? What do you want to do in the future?

c) Have you ever travelled abroad? Where did you go?

d) What did you study? What qualifications do you have?

Exercise 25

Paragraph 1 You find out her age – she's 24.

Paragraph 2 You find out his name – Brian Macintosh.

Paragraph 3 You find out the language – Portuguese.

Paragraph 4 You find out her name – Helen Rawlings.

Exercise 26

Brian Macintosh gives an email address rather than a telephone number.

Exercise 27

Three candidates are under 35: Ann Warwick (24); Jonathan Baker (27); and Helen Rawlings (21).

Exercise 28

Brian Macintosh speaks three languages: Chinese, French and German.

Exercise 29

Positive words and phrases are: *very suitable* (paragraph 1); and *well-qualified, lot of experience, useful* (paragraph 2).

Exercise 30

Negative words and phrases are: *late, not very impressed* (paragraph 3); and *the weakest candidate, doesn't have enough experience* (paragraph 4).

Exercise 31

tidily dressed = smart

having everything ready = organised/organized

having suitable training = qualified

untidily dressed = scruffy

not arriving on time = unpunctual

making mistakes = careless

Exercise 32

It's likely that Ann Warwick or Brian Macintosh would be given the job.

Exercise 33

a) 'The' is missing from the beginning of the sentence.

b) [The]Next interview … [He was] Educated in Scotland .. [His] Name was … [You] Can contact him … [He] Has worked ..

c) [Her] Name was … [She] Studied in …

Exercise 34

Suggested answers:

a) (Can you) meet Mrs Green 6pm? / Mrs Green rang – meet at 6pm?

b) (What is) availability of product 10136 asapp? (as soon as possible please) / Find out availability of 10136 asap.

c) Office closed 1-2pm (for) lunch M-F (Monday to Friday). / Office closed 1-2pm every day.

d) Ring Mr Cox after 4pm today. 03477 870654. / Mr Cox – ring after 4pm on 03477 870654

Exercise 35

Suggested answer:

Please phone Mr Wales (Rome office) re: bad sales figures and employee worries. Available until 8pm. (16 words)

READING AND WRITING TEST 3

QUESTION 1

MODEL ANSWER

Express Printing plc Wolverstock Road
Sussex S19 8HT

18th September 2009

Products Manager
Merchant Printers
Greene's Industrial Estate
Birmingham BE9 6ME

Dear Customer,

I am pleased to introduce myself to you. My name is (Mary Porter) and I have recently joined Express Printing plc, where I am looking forward to working with you.

I have worked for a number of years in Sales, but Express Printing has such a good reputation for the high standard of its products that I cannot think of a better place to work.

I would like to introduce Express Printing's latest product – the XXON printer/photocopier, which is released this month. This printer is one of the fastest of its generation, with the new feature of remote control, and improved reliability.

As an already-valued customer we would like to offer you the chance to see and use this product for yourself. We offer you the super-efficient XXON printer with 20% off and immediate, free delivery. Both offers are only available this month.

In addition, we would like to include 6 months' service and installation – all at no charge.

Please contact me on my direct line (0172 911108) to take advantage of this offer, and feel free to pass this information on to any of your clients who may also be interested in our company.

I hope to hear from you soon.

Yours sincerely,

(Mary Porter)

Sales Executive

(190 words)

QUESTION 2

Quotes are suggested answers only, and other wording might be acceptable.

1	TRUE	gloomy picture/ facing severe economic problems
2	FALSE	producer of batteries/ Russian investor
3	TRUE	petrol engine/domestic electricity mains
4	FALSE	near development site/ worldwide 3 years
5	FALSE	as yet unnamed/ adapting its products
6	TRUE	cost about £15,000/ similar worldwide price
7	TRUE	held up/ concerns about safety
8	TRUE	big international manufacturers / next week's show
9	TRUE	expertise with batteries/ adapting for car
10	TRUE	economic problems/ affect labour market

QUESTION 3

1 (over) 5,000
2 filing cabinet
3 executive chair
4 computer keyboard
5 2
6 396124
7 8 pm
8 2
9 Kaski's
10 5% discount / discount
11 computer keyboard
12 £10
13 0800 0221133
14 leather
15 any time
16 5%
17 filing cabinet
18 7
19 2
20 £15

QUESTION 4

NAME	DATE OF VISIT	ARRIVAL TIME	LUNCH DETAILS	IN CHARGE OF VISIT
1 MR CHOI	WEDNESDAY 16TH	1000	1300 – VEGETARIAN	MS WELLS
2 MR ALLSOP	WEDNESDAY 16TH	1215	1330	MR JENKINS
3 MR SVENSSON	MONDAY (14TH)	1030	WORKING LUNCH	MS WELLS
4 MR ANDERSSON	THURSDAY (17TH)	0900	1230 – LIGHT LUNCH ONLY	MR COOMBS

READING AND WRITING TEST 3
Further practice and guidance

Exercise 1
You want to encourage your readers to read the information and contact you, so the best way to do this would be to use an enthusiastic and friendly style, rather than giving lots of facts and being too formal.

Exercise 2
Useful words:

Versatile, portable, lightweight, stylish, reliable, useful, indispensable.

Exercise 3
a) expensive

b) unreliable

c) computer crash

d) complicated

Exercise 4
You have to include four points in the letter.

Exercise 5
a) no charge

b) improved reliability

c) immediate delivery

d) good reputation

e) a number of years

f) already-valued customer

g) latest

Exercise 6
The meeting, which is **compulsory** for all members of staff, will take place on Monday 21 August. We wish to improve relations with our **already-valued customers** and **resolve** some recent problems which have happened.

Please **confirm** that you can attend the meeting, and do not **hesitate** to **contact** me if there are any problems.

Exercise 7
Possible answers:

Positive: bright (news)

Negative: gloomy (picture); severe economic problems

Exercise 8
Possible answers:

Newtown Arena – the location of the International Car Show where the hybrid car will be presented for the first time.

Asian – the nationality of the car manufacturer who has come up with the hybrid car.

Russian – the tycoon who has invested in the Asian car company is said to be Russian.

Exercise 9
Possible answers:

1 – 1-litre petrol engine (paragraph 4)

85 – 85km is the distance the car can travel when fully charged (paragraph 5)

15,000 – the car will be sold for about £15,000 (paragraph 6)

3 – the car will be sold worldwide within 3 years.

Exercise 10
a) hybrid (paragraph 2)

b) heavily (paragraph 3)

c) fully (paragraph 5)

d) revealed (paragraph 7)

e) capitalized (on) (paragraph 7)

Exercise 11
You should have highlighted: *4-door, electric motor, (1-litre) petrol engine.*

Exercise 12
Examples of the present perfect are 'has come up with', 'have been fighting (paragraph 2); 'has only recently joined', 'has already invested' (paragraph 3); and 'has capitalized on' and 'has held up' (paragraph 7).

Exercise 13

Words often used with the present perfect are 'already' and 'recently'.

Exercise 14

a) He travels to work by bus every day. (present simple)

b) The Department worked efficiently last month. (past simple)

c) The bass was having a meeting during his lunch break. (past continuous)

d) She is visiting the Rome office at the moment. (present continuous)

e) The company has sold lots of televisions this year. (present perfect simple)

Exercise 15

There are normally 20 questions and four pieces of product information / four products.

Exercise 16

18 of the questions begin with question words. *How many/ much* requires a number; *which* requires a name; *what* requires a name or a fact; *why* requires a reason and *when* requires a date or time.

Exercise 17

a) 1 b) 1 c) 2 d) 1 e) 1 f) 1

Exercise 18

Figures are mentioned in four of the questions: 3, 4, 11 and 17.

Exercise 19

The offers on the right are both half-price.

Exercise 20

The leather chair and filing cabinet are both available in a choice of colours.

Exercise 21

e	g	i	k	l	m	f	x	x	a	y	q	p	s
f	h	y	l	k	l	f	i	c	z	n	p	q	a
f	h	y	l	k	l	i	i	c	z	n	p	q	a
w	p	o	f	u	b	l	z	p	y	v	m	z	s
c	o	m	p	u	t	e	r	d	d	e	f	x	m
m	o	o	c	w	t	k	g	b	n	m	x	p	p
m	u	u	a	d	p	r	e	k	l	c	s	w	i
m	o	s	b	c	d	s	e	h	t	p	l	n	v
b	k	e	y	b	o	a	r	d	g	f	s	e	n
v	d	h	e	d	a	n	l	e	c	d	s	l	k
v	j	f	j	t	c	z	x	s	c	r	e	e	n
d	j	o	p	b	c	x	m	k	g	f	s	k	m

Exercise 22

Three days are mentioned: Monday, Wednesday and Thursday.

Exercise 23

Monday: 1030
Wednesday: 1000; 1130; 1215; 1300; 1330; 1630
Thursday: 0900; 1230; 1800

Exercise 24

a)

Paragraph 1: Mr Choi and Ms Wells

Paragraph 2: Mr Smith, Mr Jenkins and Mr Allsop

Paragraph 3: Mr Svensson and Ms Wells

Paragraph 4: Mr Coombs and Mr Andersson

b) Mr Smith is coming to see your boss, so no arrangements are necessary for him.

Exercise 25

a) vegetarian; appointment

b) arrangements

c) unavailable

d) co-operation

Exercise 26

a) You can *have* an appointment; you can also *make* an appointment.

b) You *make* arrangements.

c) You can *organize* as well as *arrange* something.

Exercise 27

a) I would like to **confirm** my flight (reservation) to Stockholm tomorrow.

b) The company wants to **promote its new products** all over the world.

c) Our company **does business with** other international companies.

d) 'Sorry, he's not at his desk at the moment. You can **leave a message**. / Would you like to **leave a message**?'

e) 'We would like to **place an order**.'

Exercise 28

a) impossible

b) unsatisfactory

c) illegal

d) impolite

e) discontinued

f) unlucky

g) invisible

h) misunderstand

Exercise 29

a) unsatisfactory

b) illegal

c) discontinued

d) misunderstand

e) impolite

f) impossible

g) unlucky

h) invisible

READING AND WRITING TEST 4

QUESTION 1

MODEL ANSWER

J L P Computing Services Station Road Harlow
Essex SS20 3AB

27th July 2009

IT Manager
ATT Insurance
Westgate
York Y50 1DD

Dear Customer,

Thank you for your recent letter. We are very sorry to hear that you have been experiencing some problems with our latest software package.

Unfortunately, it would appear that there is a problem with the program, which we are working hard to solve.

We would like to take this opportunity to apologize for any inconvenience caused, and we will send a service engineer to you, at your convenience, to reinstall the program and, if necessary, replace the computer itself.

Additionally, we would like to offer you 1 year's free servicing on all equipment already supplied by us to you, and a 10% discount on your next order.

Please contact me on my direct line (0932 876890) or email (p.barker@jlpcomps) to let me know a suitable time for us to visit your IT Department.

As a valued customer, we would like to reassure you that we do not take these problems lightly, and we will be taking further steps in quality control to ensure that such difficulties do not arise again.

Yours sincerely,

(Peter Barker)

Customer Relations

(173 words)

QUESTION 2

Quotes are suggested answers only, and other wording might be acceptable.

1 TRUE   explain terms clearly/ check their policy
2 FALSE   useful services/ help or repairs
3 FALSE   they must purchase/ always available
4 FALSE   confidential/ recorded for security purposes
5 TRUE   all contact information / at a glance
6 TRUE   right to cancel/ within 14 days
7 FASLSE   arrange for repairs/ storm damage
8 FALSE   two important areas/ all contact details
9 FALSE   optional/ purchase when you buy insurance
10 TRUE   number of ways/ in writing

QUESTION 3

 1 Beacon Electric
 2 £15
 3 Beacon Electric
 4 Allpower
 5 Gasline
 6 £20
 7 Beacon Electric
 8 Gasline
 9 on paper or online
10 Nothing (with 1 month's notice)
11 Allpower/Beacon Electric/Express
12 Allpower
13 Beacon Electric
14 CostLess
15 Gasline/Beacon Electric
16 Allpower
17 1 month/2 months
18 Beacon Electric
19 a 1-month penalty
20 (to get a) discount

QUESTION 4

COMPANY	DAY AND TIME	CONTACT PERSON	CONTACT DETAILS	YOUR DESTINATION
1 SOLUTIONS	MONDAY 1800	JOHN SMITH	UNKNOWN	METROPOLITAN HOTEL
2 SJODEN'S	TUESDAY 1015	MR JAMESON	0044 5621078	OFFICE IN DENVER STREET
3 NEWIDEAS.COM	THURSDAY 1300	MS LIVINGSTON	EMAIL	NEWIDEASUSA OFFICES IN SAN FRANCISCO
4 UNKNOWN	FRIDAY 0830	MR FELLOWS	PHONE	THE ELVET HOTEL, DARTINGTON SQUARE

READING AND WRITING TEST 4
Further practice and guidance

Exercise 1
a) Sorry!
b) I am very sorry.
c) We must apologize for these problems.
d) We regret this mistake.
e) We regret the inconvenience caused.

Exercise 2
a) Dear Sir / Yours faithfully / Suitable for a letter to your new bank.
b) Dear Fred / See you soon / Suitable for a letter to a friend.
c) Dear Mr Smith / Yours sincerely / Suitable for a letter to a customer.

Exercise 3
a) goods
b) products
c) items
d) computers
e) program
f) printer

Exercise 4
a) unavoidable
b) refund
c) delay

Exercise 5
a) Am
b) Br
c) Am
d) Br
e) Br
f) Am
g) Am
h) Br
i) Br
j) Am
k) Am
l) Br

Exercise 6
sidewalk = pavement
gas/gasoline = petrol
elevator = lift
fall (part of the year) = autumn
to stand in line = queue
subway = tube / underground

Exercise 7
American words/phrases: truck; area code; call collect; Monday through Friday; color; catalog; gear shift

British words/phrases: van/lorry; dialling code; reverse charges; Monday to Friday; colour; catalogue; gears

Exercise 8
Thank you for your **recent** email. We are disappointed to hear that you are **dissatisfied** with our product.

We would like the opportunity to discuss this with you. Please **contact** our office at your earliest **convenience** to arrange an **appointment** with our Sales Manager, who will be pleased to meet you.

Exercise 9
You should have highlighted words and phrases in the letter.

Exercise 10
There are six paragraphs in the text. The first and last letters of each paragraph are: I/ r; M/s; A/e; T/y; B/ e; T/s.

Exercise 11
'Insurance' is used three times, in paragraphs one (twice) and three.
'Customer/s' is used 12 times, once or more in each paragraph.

Exercise 12
Paragraph 1: (Be very careful to) explain terms clearly …
Paragraph 2: Make sure the customer knows …
Paragraph 3: Remind customers …
Paragraph 4: advise them to check …
Paragraph 5: Check they have received …
Paragraph 6: Remind the customers …

Exercise 13
Suggested answer:
Generally, the employees must make sure that the customer knows all the services available, and how to access them.

Exercise 14
Adding 'please' and the phrase 'would you mind' makes requests more polite.

Exercise 15
Suggested answers:
a) Complete the/a report by 5pm.
b) Visit the/a customer by the end of the week.
c) Arrive on time in the mornings.
d) Install a new program on the computer.
e) Arrange a flight to Copenhagen.

Exercise 16
Paragraph 1 Would you mind explaining the terms clearly …

Paragraph 2 Would you mind making sure the customer knows …

Paragraph 3 Would you mind reminding customers …

Paragraph 4 Would you mind advising them to check …

Paragraph 5 Would you mind checking they have received …

Paragraph 6 Would you mind reminding the customers …

Exercise 17

Suggested answers:

a) sudden serious situation

b) have a choice

c) buy

d) to the point

e) look at quickly

f) take away permission

Exercise 18

Two services are mentioned: Home Emergency in paragraph 2 and Advice Line on Legal Matters in paragraph 3. Only the Advice Line is optional.

Exercise 19

Each service includes the following: Home Emergency – help or repairs to home, for example storm or water damage or drainage problems (paragraph 2), and Advice Line on Legal Matters – confidential advice on any personal legal subject (paragraph 3).

Exercise 20

You are interested in home energy: gas and electricity.

Exercise 21

The four companies and their plans are: Gasline + Click 6; Allpower + Fixed Energy; Beacon Electric + Energy Plus; and Express + CostLess.

Exercise 22

Gasline sells only gas; Allpower sells gas and electricity; Beacon Electricity sells only electricity. There is no extra information given about Express.

Exercise 23

Pay monthly with Gasline; pay every three months with Allpower; pay monthly with Beacon Electric; and pay monthly or every three months with Express.

Exercise 24

a) £1057 is the cost of gas for one year with Gasline.

b) 6 is Click 6, which is Gasline's plan.

c) 3 is the number of bedrooms used in Gasline's and Express' information; and you can pay Allpower every three months.

Exercise 25

a) penalty

b) cancellation

c) online

d) discount

Exercise 26

a) fixed

b) discount

c) cancellation

d) fee

e) benefit

f) penalty

g) (give) notice

Exercise 27

Suggested answers:

Monday 1800 opening of Exhibition

Tuesday 1015 pick up from hotel to office on Denver Street

Thursday 1300 meet to go to NewIdeas.com offices

Friday 0830 taxi to take you to a breakfast meeting with Mr Fellows

Exercise 28

a) am going to write / 'going to' future

b) has made / present perfect simple

c) were / past simple

d) was talking / past continuous

e) crashes / present simple

f) am having / present continuous

Exercise 29

There are two addresses mentioned: Mr Jameson's offices on Denver Street; and Mr Fellows Hotel, the Elvet, on Dartington Square.

Exercise 30

There are three companies mentioned: Solutions (John Smith); Sjoden's (Mr Jameson); and NewIdeas.com (Ms Livingston).

Exercise 31

You do not have to write anything about transport arrangements (paragraphs 2,3 and 4).

Exercise 32

Suggested answers:

'by the way' (paragraph 1)

'don't forget … will you?' (paragraph 2)

'early start' (paragraph 4)

'head to' (paragraph 4)

Exercise 33

Suggested answers:

'By the way' could be written more formally as 'for your information', or 'in addition'.

'Don't forget … will you?' could be written more formally as 'Please remember to …' or 'Please do not forget to'.

'Friday will be an early start' could be written more formally as 'Friday starts early'.

'Head to' could be written more formally as 'travel (back) to'.

Exercise 34

Negative statements are followed by positive tags, and positive statements are followed by negative tags.

Exercise 35

a) Business has improved, **hasn't it**?

b) The market is very slow today, **isn't it**?

c) You don't like the new product, **do you**?

d) The flight was very late, **wasn't it**?

e) The new boss will attend the meeting today, **won't he/she**?

Exercise 36

a) visa

b) check in

c) passport

d) customs

e) scheduled flight

LISTENING TEST 1

PART 1

1 B	6 A
2 A	7 B
3 A	8 B
4 B	9 A
5 C	10 A

PART 2

11 C	16 B	21 D	26 A
12 D	17 A	22 A	27 A
13 A	18 B	23 C	28 D
14 B	19 C	24 B	29 B
15 D	20 B	25 B	30 B

LISTENING TEST 1
Further practice and guidance

PART 1

Exercise 1

The verbs are *I'm doing, I'm working* and *I'm hoping*. The verb form is present continuous, so probably refers to an action or event happening at or around the moment of speaking.

Exercise 2

The missing words are:

works /(Present) continuous/ was speaking / Past simple / have been increasing / Present perfect simple / am going to complete / am flying / will give

Exercise 3

Questions 1 and 3 refer to events going on at the time of speaking.

Exercise 4

Questions 4, 6, 7, 9 and 10 have verb forms for events which always or regularly happen.

Exercise 5

a) a place

b) a time

c) a person

d) an explanation

Exercise 6

a) 1

b) 4

c) 2

d) 3

e) 5

f) 6

Exercise 7

Who questions: 4 and 7 – The answer will probably be a person's name.

What questions: 6 – The answer will probably be an object or piece of information.

When questions: 8 – The answer will probably be a time or a date.

Where questions: 1 – The answer will probably be a place. 5 is an indirect 'where' question.

How questions : 3 and 9 – the answer will probably be an amount (e.g. *How much*) or an explanation.

Exercise 8

a) Yes, I have.

b) No, I didn't.

c) No, I don't.

d) Yes, I was.

e) No, I haven't.

PART 2

Exercise 1

A company could have problems with debt or its staff, or maybe a product it has produced is not working properly.

Exercise 2

B is a positive answer: 'the company sells more than 100 products'.

Exercise 3

C seems less relevant: 'the two brothers'.

Exercise 4

Answers A and D seem to be possible answers.

Exercise 5

Question 11: B (the figure is too small so would be unlikely to appear in the news)

Question 16: A, D (these options do not answer the question appropriately)

Question 27: C (it is unlikely that a company director would never travel abroad)

Exercise 6

a) fifty
b) fifteen
c) fifteen thousand
d) eleven thousand, five hundred and fifty-five
e) five hundred and thirty-five

Exercise 7

a) 355,000
b) 450
c) 62,000
d) 25,000,000
e) 38,003

Exercise 8

'0' can be written as *zero* or *nought*. You could also, but less usually, answer *nothing*; *nil* is used in football scores; *love* is used in tennis.

Exercise 9

a) wallet
b) insurance
c) economy
d) interest rates
e) bank charges
f) account
g) stock exchange
h) investment
i) cash
j) cheque
k) currency

LISTENING TEST 2

PART 1

1 B	6 A
2 A	7 A
3 B	8 B
4 C	9 B
5 B	10 C

PART 2

11 A	16 A	21 D	26 B
12 C	17 A	22 A	27 B
13 C	18 C	23 C	28 A
14 B	19 B	24 C	29 B
15 D	20 C	25 D	30 A

LISTENING TEST 2
Further practice and guidance

PART 1

Exercise 1

a) half past five in the morning; five thirty a.m. / in the morning
b) five forty-five in the morning / a.m., quarter to six in the morning
c) eight thirty in the morning / a.m., half past eight in the morning
d) eleven fifteen in the morning / a.m., quarter past eleven in the morning

Exercise 2

a) accommodation
b) address
c) ✔
d) received
e) separate
f) ✔
g) ✔
h) ✔

Exercise 3

Your initials are the first letters of your first name and surname in capitals.

PART 2

Exercise 1

Question 13: From the question and possible answers, the listening is probably about problems suffered by an oil company, causing it to be sold.

Question 15: The listening is probably about a bag.

Question 19: The conversation is probably about what to do on holiday or during free time, or planning a day out.

Question 20: The listening is probably about a celebrity's company.

Exercise 2

a) 13B
b) 23A
c) 16D
d) 22C
e) 18B
f) 20D
g) 21D

h) 17A

i) 30A

j) 26C

Exercise 3

Suggested answers

a) 12, 17, 26

b) 15

c) 18, 22

d) 13, 14, 24

e) 16, 19, 21, 28, 30

Exercise 4

a) criticize (11C)

b) celebrity (11D, 20)

c) colleague (17D, 28A)

d) branch (27A)

e) prepare (26A)

f) recommend (24)

g) benefit (27)

Exercise 5

a) The phrase 'work in' is used in all answers.

b) The word 'money' appears in all answers.

c) Options A and B start with 'He' and options C and D start with 'It'.

d) C seems unlikely: a bag can't organize work for you.

e) D seems unlikely: it is not sensible to encourage people to use more energy.

Exercise 6

a) Question 25

b) Question 14

c) Question 24

d) Question 15

Exercise 7

a) suggest

b) urge

c) persuade

d) advise

e) encourage

Exercise 8

a) suggested

b) urged

c) encouraged / persuaded (both acceptable)

d) persuade / encourage (both acceptable)

e) advised

SPEAKING TEST 1
Further practice and guidance

Exercise 1

a) You have five minutes to prepare for the test.

b) There are two parts to the Speaking test: the opening questions the examiner asks you about yourself (the warm-up), and the discussion of a subject based around a picture.

c) No, you don't have to write anything, the test is speaking only.

d) The examiner chooses the subject you will talk about.

Exercise 2

Suggested answers:

Where are you from? Where do you live? Do you like it there? What do you do? Why did you choose that job/ course? Why are you studying English? What are your ambitions?

Exercise 3

It's a good idea to give full answers, rather than short, one-word ones. For example, 'Where are you from?' could be answered with 'I come from X, which is a small city in the north of the country. I grew up there.' Fuller answers make you sound more confident and give the examiner a good impression of your speaking skills.

Exercise 4

Suggested answers:

I'm going to study hard and make sure I get a good degree. I'm going to arrange work experience for the summer holiday so I can improve my chances of getting a job and find out more about the kind of business I'm interested in. I think studying English is an excellent way of helping me improve my career prospects, and I'm going to practise as much as I can.

Exercise 5

Suggested answers:

I worked in my uncle's shop during the summer holiday, selling fruit and vegetables. I really enjoyed talking to the customers and learning how a real business worked. It was quite hard work and the hours were long, but it was a great experience.

Exercise 6

Suggested answers:

Commuting is expensive, it's bad for the environment and can add extra hours to your day.

Exercise 7

Suggested answers:

City: exciting, fun, full of opportunities, crowded, expensive

Countryside: relaxing, beautiful, boring, empty

Exercise 8

Suggested answers:

Tired, stressed, busy, hard-working, ambitious, successful.

Exercise 9

a) train

b) tube

c) car

d) bike

e) subway

f) foot

Exercise 10

Suggested answers:

Jobs in big cities are normally better paid than in small towns, and there are more kinds of work and better job prospects. Living in the suburbs is usually cheaper than living in the city, and the suburbs are considered better for bringing up children.

SPEAKING TEST 2
Further practice and guidance

Exercise 1

The warm-up lasts two minutes.

Exercise 2

a) pen

b) stapler

c) hole punch

d) file / folder / ringbinder

e) (computer) keyboard

f) (computer) screen

Exercise 3

Suggested answers:

a) traffic, pedestrians, shops

b) smart clothes, technology, stationary

c) tables and chairs, waiter/waitress, cutlery

Exercise 4

Suggested answers:

In the morning I usually get up early, have a shower, have my breakfast and catch the bus to work.

In the afternoon I sometimes go to a café for lunch, and read the newspaper.

In the evening I like to meet my friends or stay at home and watch television.

Exercise 5

Suggested answers:

Positive: useful, fun, helpful

Negative: expensive, distracting, unreliable

Exercise 6

a) and

b) because

c) However

d) also

e) but

Exercise 7

a) and

b) but

c) however

d) because

e) also

Exercise 8

Suggested answers:

Technology – such as computers, mp3 players and mobile phones – is useful **and** fun to use, **but** it can **also** distract us from work **because** we would rather surf the internet or chat to our friends. Also, new technology can be expensive, especially if you want the latest gadgets. **However**, they can be very helpful in finding information we need for work or study.

RECORDING SCRIPT

LCCI LISTENING TEST 1

PART 1

1   Where are you working?
    A: I'm doing some business exams.
    B: I'm working in the buyer's office.
    C: I'm hoping to get a job soon.

2   Have you seen Mr Smith this morning?
    A: Yes, he left about an hour ago.
    B: No, he's the Sales Manager.
    C: His desk is on the left.

3   How are you doing?
    A: Fine, thanks.
    B: I can't find the report you wanted.
    C: I'm reading this report.

4   Who is in charge of the department?
    A: No, there is no charge.
    B: It's Charles Armstrong.
    C: The department deals with customer complaints.

5   Do you know where the report is?
    A: I haven't read it yet.
    B: It's very interesting.
    C: It still hasn't arrived.

6   What are your initials, please?
    A: J W
    B: Julian Williams
    C: Mr Williams

7   Who do I need to speak to?
    A: I'm sorry, he's not here.
    B: Mr Smythson can help you.
    C: There's no-one.

8   When is the next train to London, please?
    A: It's on platform 15.
    B: It's at 5 o'clock.
    C: Change at Haywards Heath, platform 5.

9   How much does it cost?
    A: It's free.
    B: It's 1 mile.
    C: There's a lot.

10 Can I exchange my money here?
    A: Yes. What would you like?
    B: Sorry, I don't have any change.
    C: This dress is too small.

PART 2

11
Radio Interviewer: Tell us about the latest situation in the United States.

Correspondent: Not good news from here, I'm afraid: three million jobs could be lost in a year if America's 'Big Three' car makers are allowed to collapse. Even if only one of the companies crashes, tens of thousands of people will lose their jobs.

12
Announcer: … and now over to our City editor for Company news.

City Editor: Smith and Smith Ltd., owned by two brothers, have made profits of £8 million. The company has had problems with its bank, but the brothers employ more than 100 members of staff and its products are continuing to sell well.

13
Radio advert: Save with us – we offer the best interest rates in town this autumn! You must have an opening balance of £1,000, and leave the money with us until June 1 next year. Come and join us!

14
Interviewer: What advice would you give to DIY enthusiasts?

Expert: Well, with not much money to spare, it's still nice to smarten up your home at holiday time, or before relatives come to stay, so here are some tips on how to give your house a face-lift with a budget of only £100.

15
Friend 1: You don't look very happy. What's the matter?

Friend 2: Well, I've had to cancel a holiday. I sent all the details to my insurance company three months ago, but whenever I phone them, I only get a recorded message, so I can't get through. I'm becoming quite concerned about it.

16
Interviewer: Can you give us some tips about shopping at this time of year?

Expert: Well, shopping for presents is always expensive, but looking on the Internet can help you find the best prices for computer games, DVDs, toys and books. You can save up to 15 per cent if you are careful, and sometimes the goods are also delivered free.

17

Interviewer: How much cash do you usually have on you?

Celebrity: Today, I've got £10 in my pocket, and 40 American dollars in my wallet. I travel a lot, so I usually have different kinds of money on me. I try not to carry too much money, but some cash is always useful, for instance, when you need to get a taxi.

18

Speaker: The pound was worth more than $4 in 1944, but it has fallen to $1.45 since then. The fall of the pound is seen as a way to rebalance and help the economy. Many banks think that the pound will recover because of recent interest rate cuts.

19

Client: Can you explain my right to paid holidays?

Lawyer: By law, every employee in the UK has the right to a paid holiday, from their first day at work. Most employees in the UK have just under five weeks' paid holidays every year. There are also a number of public holidays. Employers do not have to pay their staff for time off on public holidays, but many companies do.

20

Friend 1: Why aren't you happy with your bank?

Friend 2: Well, last month I paid some money into the wrong bank account – I made an error when I typed in the account number. Unfortunately, my bank hasn't been very helpful about getting my money back. I know it was my fault, but I still think the bank should try to help me.

21

Man: I'm very concerned. I sent a cheque for £700 to my bank, to be invested, but three months later I've still not heard from them, even though I've written three letters. If I send another cheque though, I'll lose the interest that I should have earned by now on the investment.

22

Interviewer: So, tell me about your early career.

Business man: Well, first I trained as an accountant, and I met Tony Smith soon after.

He hired me as his personal financial adviser, to sort out his tax and financial difficulties. Together we set up our company in 1994 and we haven't looked back since, although it has been hard work. The first two years were perhaps the hardest, but now we've got the formula right.

23

Newsreader: Jetaway's results for last year show that 35 new planes were added to the fleet, and passenger numbers were up 15 per cent. Revenue was up by twice this amount, to 30 per cent. However, the rising cost of fuel has been a major concern, and overall profits have fallen by 46 per cent – from £202 million to £110 million.

24

Interviewer: Could you explain to us what is happening in the money lending market at the moment?

Financial expert: Because interest rates are going down – for example by 0.5 per cent last month – a person will save £48 a month on the average mortgage of £200,000. But in future months, you might not have to pay any interest at all on your loan, if the bank rate falls low enough. This means you would simply continue to make capital repayments.

25

Speaker: A new branch of JSN opened recently, here in Georgetown. One of the most successful chain stores worldwide – there are over 7,800 branches – it is run by two of the most secretive brothers you can imagine! Neither of them has appeared publicly for the last 40 years, and even their most senior staff claim never to have met them. Occasionally, however, there are rumours that they have been spotted in one of their stores, checking the shelves and arranging the products.

26

Radio advert: We offer listeners a chance to experience the beauty of the Bay of Naples and the Amalfi Coast. You will travel along the coast, visit the sights, and stay in a three or four-star hotel. Included are return flights from various airports; seven nights half-board; and guided sightseeing with a tour manager. Prices given are for two people sharing a room – singles are available at a supplement.

27

Interviewer: So, what is your typical working day like?

Company Director: Well, I get up about 7 a.m. and catch the bus to my office before nine. I don't know how many other company bosses there are on the bus, as there's not a lot of conversation! A typical day is usually full of meetings, either in person or by videoconferencing around the world. I leave the office at about 6 p.m., and do paperwork in the evenings. I also travel for two weeks in every four.

28

Speaker: The company was founded in London in 1884 to provide insurance and loans to ordinary people. It expanded rapidly by selling policies to businesses. The company moved into its world-famous red brick building in 1899 and stayed there until 2005, when it moved to more modern premises nearby. Today, the company employs more than 2,800 people full-time at its head office, and has more than 21 million customers all over the world.

29

Announcer: … and now for some positive company news. Baasom, the luxury fashion house, has shown a small increase in its operating profits. Experts forecast that first half-year earnings will be between 90 to 98 million pounds. The company is about to open new stores in London and Los Angeles, and benefits from the global appeal of its luxury items.

30

Radio advert: Did you know you can save up to £100 on newspapers over the year? Just look at our special 25 per cent off offer! All you have to do is phone 0800 069 2387 and register, quoting D209. This offer does not include home delivery, and you must subscribe for at least 24 weeks. Hurry – you have just two weeks to register before the offer ends!

LCCI LISTENING TEST 2

PART 1

1 Have you seen my diary?
   A: No, I haven't done it.
   B: Isn't it on your desk?
   C: I want to read it.

2 Please spell your name for me.
   A: S-C-H-M-I-D-T
   B: I'm Mr Schmidt.
   C: I don't know.

3 What time is Mr Healy coming to the office?
   A: He's always late.
   B: He usually comes at half past nine.
   C: He doesn't.

4 What's your job?
   A: It's very interesting.
   B: not at the moment
   C: It's to do with banking.

5 When does Mr Bystrom's flight arrive?
   A: Terminal 5
   B: Five thirty a.m., I think.
   C: London, Heathrow

6 Who is the CEO of the company?
   A: Mr Neville
   B: nobody
   C: since 1990

7 What's your plan for the meeting?
   A: To listen to the other ideas first.
   B: I have no ideas to present.
   C: Eleven people will attend.

8 What's the charge for this service?
   A: Mr Reeves
   B: It's quite reasonable.
   C: Real estate will deal with it.

9 Could you explain how to use this program?
   A: It's switched off.
   B: Yes, it's quite simple.
   C: It's produced by Microsoft.

10 Are you available for a meeting at 1030?
   A: The meeting always starts at 1030.
   B: I don't know where the meeting is.
   C: Yes, certainly.

PART 2

11

TV reporter: The International Bank, which recently received help from the government, has hired a number of celebrities to entertain customers as part of a sponsorship plan. This information has angered many senior government ministers and there is widespread criticism of their action. The Bank is one of the world's biggest sports sponsors.

12

Interviewer: So, tell us why you got involved with the Berriedale closure.

Celebrity: I asked Berriedale to reverse its decision to close its manufacturing plant because I know how hard its employees work, and I lived near the factory in Wales when I was growing up. If I hadn't made a success of singing, I'd probably be working there now!

13

Presenter: The well-known French family of Tillac has put its oil company up for sale, in an attempt to raise cash after problems with its global investments. The sale could raise 500 million pounds for the German-based company. A number of other companies, including Tillac's Japanese partner company and an oil company from Abu Dhabi, have already shown interest in the sale.

14

Friend 1: I want to start saving money. Do you have any ideas?

Friend 2: Well, I saw an advert in the paper recently, which looked interesting. It said that with a cashback credit card you can get money back on your everyday spending – up to five per cent in the first six months, or as much as £200 – and you don't have to pay a fee to have the card.

15

Colleague 1: What can we get for John's leaving present? I've got about £50.

Colleague 2: Well, I saw a really useful briefcase in town last week. You know his desk is always in a mess, so it might be perfect for him – it's got a padded computer pocket with a security lock, an organizer pocket, a compartment for files, and exterior pockets. It's really light, and is the right size to take on flights, too. Best of all, it's only £40.

16

Friend 1: Have you tried that new supermarket near your house, yet? It looks good.

Friend 2: Yes, it is. I went there last week after I read an article about it. They've added 8,000 articles to their range of products, they bake their bread onsite, the fruit and vegetable counters are laid out like a market, and, of course, they're really cheap!

17

Interviewer: Why do men seem to have more problems than women when they lose their job?

Expert: Men tend to see their job as a big part of their identity, so they feel ashamed and depressed if they lose it. However, women often see the same situation as an opportunity to catch up with things, especially if they have children.

18

Presenter: Can you tell us about some of the differences between the US and the UK magazine markets?

Expert: Yes, I can. Some interesting facts are that sales of American magazines went down last year by 11 per cent, but it was a better picture in the UK, where sales actually increased by about five per cent. That means a spectacular 82 million magazines are being read in the UK each year! One men's magazine has seen a 15 per cent drop in sales, and home improvement magazines are also down, but on the other hand, cookery magazines are a major growth area.

19

Friend 1: Do you fancy going out this weekend?

Friend 2: Good idea. I was looking on a website yesterday, and found some fantastic deals. There's £9 off tickets for that play about the French singer – I can't remember her name – and a couple of offers for theatre-break hotel packages. One show we thought about going to see – *Men in White* – has got 70 per cent off ticket prices, and there's also a good offer for cheap tickets with a meal afterwards.

20

Interviewer: Why have you sold part of your stake in your production company?

Celebrity: It's the right time, and I was happy with the television company I was selling it to. I know the two companies can co-operate well with each other, and we've secured a long-term future by doing this. I'm also 4 million pounds better off!

21

Woman: I had some good news today. I'm going to get some money repaid by my electricity company.

Man: That's great. Now you can take that holiday! I told you the company had overcharged you. It's a good job that you contacted them and complained, otherwise they would have kept the money.

22

Radio advert: Energy bills are a really big expense for most homes – for example, last year they rose by an average of 44 per cent. Channel 10 has teamed up with Energyline to create an exclusive service to help our viewers switch energy companies – helping you to save up to £400 a year. Call today on 0900 870 33 88 to register, giving XJ910 as your reference number.

23

Interviewer: So why has the supermarket been criticized for its packaging?

Spokesman: We think that comparisons have not been made fairly, with different sizes of products being compared across different supermarkets. Also, only pre-packed products were compared, while 25 per cent of our sales are over the counter.

24

Colleague 1: My bank's made another mistake. I must change my account.

Colleague 2: Why don't you join mine? They always say 'satisfaction is certain' and guess what? You'll get money in your account if you're happy after six months, and twice that amount if you decide to move your account again.

25

Colleague 1: I'm getting really stressed about this work. What can I do?

Colleague 2: Well, I belong to the staff health and fitness club. It's open after work until 10 p.m., and there's a really good variety of activities to try, ranging from swimming to training in the gym. It works for me.

26

Colleague 1: You didn't get the promotion, then?

Colleague 2: No, I was really disappointed, but the boss said they wanted to look for 'new blood' and employ somebody from outside. I wish they'd decided that before, though. Then I wouldn't have spent so much time preparing for the interview!

27

Friend 1: Shall we go to Deep South?

Friend 2: That's a good idea! I was reading the other day about their future plans – they're going to open about 250 new restaurants in the UK in the next five years. They say that because each branch employs about 25 people, there would be lots of new jobs, and they're also going to spend 90 million pounds improving the restaurants they've got already.

28

Colleague 1: Have you seen the advertisement for Secretary of the Year?

Colleague 2: Yes. I thought we might nominate Chris for it. You've got to be very organized and focused on your job, as well as really good with people, and full of motivation. What do you think?

29

Man: I'm looking for a post in the banking industry.

HR Manager: Rockton Bank has just started recruiting, and they're looking for people with just your experience. It has a number of special offers and loans for customers at the moment, so sales advisors are needed urgently.

30

Student 1: Are you going to the Job Fair? It looks really useful, now that we've taken all our exams. It's free, and they say they show you how to write a CV and give a presentation. Some big firms are going to attend, too.

Student 2: Sounds like a good idea. Where do we register?

1.01   Test 1 Part 1:   Instructions and example question

1.02–1.11   Test 1 Part 1:   Questions 1-10

1.12   Test 1 Part 2:   Instructions and example question

1.13–1.32   Test 1 Part 2:   Questions 11-30

1.33   Test 2 Part 1:   Instructions and example question

1.34–1.43   Test 2 Part 1:   Questions 1-10

1.44   Test 2 Part 2:   Instructions and example question

1.45–1.64   Test 2 Part 2:   Questions 11-30

1.65   Credits